ADVANCED
PROPERTY
DEVELOPMENT

DEDICATION

This book is dedicated to my soul mate and amazing wife, Britta Wallwork, and to my amazing, always positive family Siènna, Skyla, and Silàs. Thank you, Britta, for believing in me always and without question, right from the outset. We will always dream big and continue to enjoy every moment as though it's our last.

ADVANCED PROPERTY

DEVELOPMENT

TURN YOUR PASSION FOR PROPERTY INVESTING INTO A FULL-TIME CAREER

NICHOLAS WALLWORK

Produced by www.extraordinarymillionaire.com

71-75 Shelton Street
Covent Garden
London
WC2H 9JQ

View the full range of mindset and
wealth-building books and courses at

www.wealthlabs.co.uk

Typesetting and publishing by UK Book Publishing

www.ukbookpublishing.com

ISBN: 978-1-916572-61-4

ABOUT THE AUTHOR

Nicholas Wallwork is a multi-millionaire property investor, developer, International *For Dummies* author, and accredited property educator and mentor. Well-known for his role on SKY TV as a property investment angel on *Property Elevator*, Nicholas has a highly respected name within the property sector and regularly appears as a property market commentator on TV, YouTube, podcasts, radio and at national property events.

Nicholas fell into property in 2002 when he realised turning his first house into a small HMO (rather than living in it himself) made complete financial sense. HMOs and commercial-to-residential development were to form key strategies of his successful property career. Aged just 25 he had no mortgage or bills to pay and could effectively retire (all be it modestly), teaching him a very early lesson that passive income from assets (property and investments) was the way to build long term wealth and a flexible, comfortable and happy lifestyle.

Today, Nicholas has developed in excess of £100million worth of UK property and is an owner in a group of successful property businesses, *Redbrick*, including a property investment consultancy, several development companies, a lettings and management business, and the ethical online Wealth education community, *Wealth Labs*.

Just like the Extraordinary Millionaire, the founders of Wealth Labs believe that for Wealth to be truly sustainable it needs to encompass and permeate all areas of life. True wealth starts in the mind. It crystalises purpose and passion, it becomes a way of life, it enables freedom, it encourages compassion, and it ensures legacy.

Any journey through life (and indeed property) is never plain sailing and Nicholas definitely faced his share of challenges. Surviving the credit crunch and covid were some of the biggest, teaching him many important lessons which he shares with you through *The Extraordinary Millionaire* books and live online courses, and his 1-2-1 mentorships - all of which are powered by **wealthlabs.co.uk**.

To be successful in any business including property you need to stay at the top of your game. This means continually educating yourself and improving your skills and knowledge to further your business and personal success. This is where online educational communities like Wealth Labs offer incredible value.

Connect with me

As you work your way through this book, I'd love to hear what you think. Which tools and techniques really resonated with you? Did some of them surprise you? What bits made you sit up and say 'Yes! That's so true.'

You can connect with me on Instagram (I'm *@nicholas_wallwork*), on LinkedIn, via my website *nicholaswallwork.com* and through Wealth Labs *www.wealthlabs.co.uk* (incidentally, this is also where you can find details about my other books, classes, coaching and mentorship programmes). I can't wait to hear from you!

INTRODUCING
WEALTH LABS

Wealth Labs is completely free to join, and offers a varied portfolio of online property training, coaching and mentorship products. Nicholas has condensed his decades of property expertise into his online courses, events and books, giving you the opportunity to learn from his successful blueprint and gain access to the very best *power team* of property professionals.

Link to online courses: https://wealth-labs.mn.co/share/IeS29tBS6t1wOVaU? utm_source=manual

Nicholas is passionate about helping others succeed in property and offers tailored 1-2-1 mentorship sessions to help people fast-track their property investment goals and make real progress. He can help you make key decisions on maximising layout and value from a property, overcome issues with planning, secure the right finance structure for your project, make the jump to larger more complex developments, move into a different strategy completely, attract private investors, navigate the construction and post-construction phases, and successfully market your finished product.

Link to mentorships: https://nicholaswallwork.com/mentorship-with-nicholas/

THE EXTRAORDINARY MILLIONAIRE

The Extraordinary Millionaire is a series of educational books and courses (this book included) which aim to inspire and motivate people to take their first steps toward becoming an *Extraordinary Millionaire*.

An Extraordinary Millionaire goes beyond focusing solely on money, emphasizing the importance of abundance in all aspects of life. They express gratitude for their current circumstances while striving for the life they desire, understanding that mindset plays a crucial role in achieving success.

The books share key training, insights and knowledge on property investment, success mindset and other wealth-building strategies, through a storytelling approach. In the books you will encounter a relatable character named George who embodies the aspirations and challenges shared by my own friends, family, and acquaintances with whom I have had conversations about breaking free from the 9-5 "rat race" and achieving financial freedom.

Harnessing the REAL tools for success outlined in these books and courses empower individuals to grow their wealth and create an extraordinary life. By adopting an abundance mindset, continuously learning, unlearning harmful money beliefs, building positive relationships, and giving back, anyone can embark on the journey to becoming an Extraordinary Millionaire.

Extraordinary Millionaire books can be purchased on Amazon.co.uk
Extraordinary Millionaire courses can be booked on WealthLabs.co.uk

ALSO BY NICHOLAS WALLWORK

The Extraordinary Millionaire

Professional Property Strategies

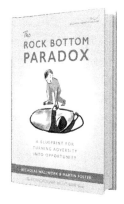

The Rock Bottom Paradox

Investing in International Real Estate For Dummies

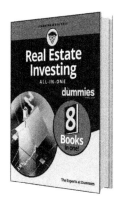

Real Estate Investing All-In-One For Dummies

Brexit For Dummies

AUTHOR'S ACKNOWLEDGMENTS

A big thank you to my team at Redbrick for helping us deliver our unique development projects and continuing to push the business forward. I'd also like to thank Tom Gillitt who is a valuable member of our extended project management team. Tom is a fantastic project manager and contracts administrator and manages a huge number of the projects we've been involved with both on our own account and for my mentorship clients' sites. Tom has also kindly contributed a substantial amount of technical knowledge to the content in this book for which I'm very grateful.

Thank you to all my personal 1-2-1 mentees and indeed all the students of WealthLabs.co.uk for your support and engagement as you all embark on your own property journeys. I'm grateful to have been able to help so many people achieve so much and seeing you do well is one of my biggest goals in life. Onwards and Upwards!

A final thank you to all our JV partners and investors who have trusted us through both the good and tough times in the market allowing us to continue to push forward creating win/win relationships in everything that we do and moving from strength to strength.

CONTENTS

CHAPTER 1

TURNING A PASSION FOR PROPERTY DEVELOPMENT INTO A FULL-TIME CAREER

Let's start with a confession. I didn't start my property career as a developer. In fact, I started as a young landlord, renting out rooms in my first home. A pretty humble start, but it was enough to get me hooked on the idea of earning an income from property. Now, with almost two decades as a full-time property investor under my belt, my portfolio has grown to incorporate a wide range of different property strategies.

One of the most rewarding of those strategies - especially in this age, when so many of our towns and cities appear to be short of high quality, affordable housing stock - is property development. Whether I'm developing an empty plot of land, or converting a vacant commercial building for residential use, I get huge personal satisfaction from delivering development projects that enhance the community and create much-needed places for people to live.

And, of course, the financial rewards can be significant. Which is probably why you picked up this book in the first place!

ALWAYS ADD VALUE

This is something of a motto of mine: always add value. It's hard to think of any strategy that embodies this more than property development. Even the smallest development project - something as simple as refurbishing a standard three-bedroom home - adds value.

This is important because smart property investors don't rely on a rising market to earn their profit. By adding value to a property, you're proactively seeking out profit and maximising your return on investment.

As your development expertise grows, and you take on bigger projects, you begin to add more and more value. The idea is your return on investment increases in line with the value you're adding. And this is how you turn property development from an on-the-side gig into a full-time career.

One of the things I love about property development - especially once you move beyond straightforward refurbishments - is that there are multiple ways to add value, such as:

- Building on an empty plot of land.
- Converting a single unit into multiple units.
- Extending a property significantly.
- Changing the use of a property. This strategy in particular has been hugely successful for me, and is one I'd recommend to anyone who wants to grow their expertise as a property developer.
- Plus, you ultimately have the choice to sell the finished product and pocket the capital growth, or keep it and rent it out for long-term income. In other words, not all property development is about selling on for a profit. The best way to create value (and meet your personal goals) might be to look to the long term and develop for income.

ABOUT YOU AS A DEVELOPER

Another thing I love about property development – aside from the potential to (say it with me) *always add value* – is that it's relatively easy to scale up. I took my first steps into property development with small refurbishments and conversions and now routinely take on multi-million-pound developments. If I can do it, so can you. I didn't start with a huge cash buffer or trust fund cushion to fall back on, and I don't for a second assume you have that luxury either.

This book is therefore written with a particular type of developer in mind – one's who's at a tipping point in their property development journey. It's not intended as a nuts-and-bolts beginner's guide. Rather, this book assumes you've got a few developments under your belt and are looking to progress from beginner to intermediate level. You're ready to take on more complex projects, scale up your activities in an achievable way, and, ultimately, turn property development into a full-time career.

(That said, this book will be useful to high net worth individuals who are looking to dive straight into property development with higher-value projects, while remaining fairly hands-off. A number of clients that I mentor fit this bill.)

This may mean you're looking to take on projects such as:

- New builds
- Splitting up a larger building into multiple units
- Converting an existing building from one use class to another (commercial-to-residential conversions being a current boom area)
- Or at the very least, a substantial alteration to an existing property

In general, then, I presume you're looking to progress beyond straightforward refurbishments, such as updating a tired family home into a nicer looking family home.

I also take the liberty of assuming that you want to earn a good portion of your income, or maybe all of your income, from property - perhaps even combining property development with other property investment strategies (more on this coming up). This was certainly my goal when I first started renting out rooms in my home. I wanted to quit the rate race - at the time, I was working all hours in the City - become my own boss and earn a comfortable living from property.

Achieving this goal required something of a mindset shift . . .

CULTIVATING A PASSIVE INCOME MINDSET

If you're ready to make the leap from someone who dabbles in property development to full-time property developer, you need to treat your property development portfolio as though it's a proper business. And as any business owner learns, a key part of success is knowing how best to spend your time.

Why you often need to take a step back to drive your business forward

Up until now, you may have been project managing your own developments, liaising with contractors and subcontractors, overseeing the schedule and managing costs all yourself. However, progressing to bigger projects means you'll have to hand off many of the day-to-day tasks involved in a project to other people. In other words, as your developments scale up, so too does the number of people you need to rely on in order to successfully complete projects.

This was a hard lesson for me to learn in the early days. It took a while for me to understand that my time wasn't well spent sourcing materials myself and being on site every day. By doing those things myself, I was saving money, right? That may be true in the short term. But it meant I was essentially working as a full-time project manager. And that wasn't my goal. My goal was to be a full-time property investor.

I don't regret being so hands-on with my early projects, and neither should you - for one thing, I learned a lot about the construction process. But something had to give. Eventually the penny dropped - I had to start working *on* my business not *in* my business. I had to start focusing on growing my portfolio and finding *the next* great development opportunity, rather than being knee-deep in the minutia of the current project.

Nowadays, I have a team of experts who help me at every stage of a development, from sourcing and assessing potential developments to navigating the pre-construction stage (design, tendering, etc.) and managing the construction itself. I call these experts my 'dream team', and I highly recommend you start building (or expanding) your own dream team. There're more about this in Chapter 3.

Introducing passive income

This is where the passive income mindset comes in. If you've heard about passive income - perhaps from books such as *Rich Dad, Poor Dad* or *The 4-Hour Work Week* - you'll know the basic principle is to maximise your return on investment while minimising your day-to-day involvement. It's about getting your money to work for you, not you working for money.

Of course, the passive income mindset isn't just about money - it's about rethinking the fundamental nature of work, and breaking free of the 9-5 grind, so that you can live life your way. Again, this is such a natural fit with property development. Chances are, like me, you were drawn to property development precisely because you want to escape the rat race and work for yourself.

Bottom line, if your goal is to grow as a property developer, you'll need to learn to relinquish many tasks and responsibilities. This applies even if you're a builder by trade. If you're serious about becoming a full-time property developer, you can't physically do every aspect of every build yourself. It's just not sustainable.

I should say that, as a developer, you're never entirely hands-off. Even with my amazing dream team, I'm still heavily involved with every project. For example, I have a project manager to manage the day-to-day construction, but I talk to the project manager most days and still attend regular on-site progress meetings. What I'm not doing is sourcing materials, liaising with the building control inspector to arrange their next inspection, or chasing the contractor for the latest programme of works. Those tasks are important, but they're not a good use of *my* time.

This book therefore walks you through the key stages and considerations of a development project, working on the assumption that you won't be doing absolutely everything yourself, but that you'll still be heavily involved.

Building multiple sources of revenue

One final point on passive income. An important part of the passive income mindset is generating multiple sources of revenue. Therefore, you might want to consider building other property investment strategies into your portfolio, alongside your developments (more on this in Chapter 10).

I've found that growing as a property developer has massively added to my success in other areas of property investing, and you may find the same thing. If you're interested in learning about other property investment strategies, you might like to check out my book *Professional Property Investment Strategies* or browse the range of educational ebooks, courses, and events available on the Wealth Labs website (which is a site I co-founded - another of the passive income strings to my bow). Head to wealthlabs.co.uk to find out more.

ABOUT THIS BOOK

We've talked about you as a developer – specifically, the assumptions I make about where you are in your property development journey and what you're looking to achieve. Now let's talk about what you can expect from this book.

As I've said, this isn't a beginner's book (although I do recognise that some novice investors with deep pockets do want to go straight into larger developments, rather than cut their teeth on smaller projects, and I've kept that in mind throughout).

This book is designed to help you level up your property development career, covering the key processes and considerations that you'll have to navigate as you take on larger and more complex developments.

Because you're less likely to be overseeing everything yourself on these sorts of projects, this isn't a step-by-step guide on how to, for example, develop an office building into an apartment block or build a new home from scratch. For reasons I've already mentioned, you'll naturally have to hand over more tasks as your projects scale up.

Therefore, this book covers what you need to know as a growing property developer, including:

- Developing for specific property strategies and the need to define your strategy before you even source a potential project.
- What sorts of tasks you can typically expect to outsource and how to build your own trusted dream team.
- The range of funding options available for developers, including creative funding options like joint venture partnerships.
- How to source deals that other developers don't know about, plus the essential thought processes that go into assessing development opportunities.
- How to navigate planning, design and other pre-construction tasks (critical to the success of more complex projects).

- How to work with a project manager to keep your projects on track.
- How to bring your projects to a successful conclusion and get the most out of sales and lettings agents.
- How to protect yourself against market swings.
- And, finally, the importance of investing in your own education as a property developer.

These are things I had to learn myself the hard way. By reading this book, you can learn from my experience, avoid some common mistakes that investors typically make when taking on more difficult projects, and (I hope), just enjoy the journey that little bit more.

A few extra things to note about this book:

- At the end of most chapters, you'll find a brief case study that highlights a key lesson related to that chapter's topic. These are all based on real developments that my company has completed – or projects where I have mentored a budding investor through the development process. (Mentoring is something I'm hugely passionate about, and you can read more about this in Chapter 11.)
- Naturally, every development project is different, so not everything in this book will apply to each of your projects. Always be guided by your dream team of experts (particularly your project manager) on what does and doesn't apply to your particular project.
- This book is written from my perspective as a developer in England. If you're based elsewhere in the UK, be aware that different rules, regulations and processes may apply.
- Finally, the examples in this book are focused on developing for residential use, as opposed to developing for commercial use. That's my particular area of expertise and a big focus for me at this point in my career. It's also a savvy strategy in general, since, at the time of writing, there's huge demand for housing in England. What's more a relaxation of planning laws means it's easier than ever to convert buildings for residential use (see Chapter 6 for more on planning).

SO WHAT TYPES OF DEVELOPMENT ARE WE TALKING ABOUT?

Property development is a broad church. The term property development can refer to anything from renovating or extending a property to converting a building from one use class to another. And with new builds, it can mean anything from building one house on a plot of land to building a giant housing estate or 30-floor skyscraper in the centre of London.

I've focused my attention here on the sorts of projects that are achievable for my intended audience - developers who already have a few developments under their belt, and are ready to take on more complex, higher value projects. It goes without saying that, at this stage in your property career, I don't recommend attempting a huge housing development or building a 30-floor skyscraper!

But converting an existing commercial building for residential use - something like a small-ish office building, a care home or even a pub - is absolutely doable at this stage in your career. As is developing a house into separate apartments. Or even building a property from scratch on a plot of land. These are the sorts of projects I had in mind when writing this book.

In a way, it doesn't matter what type of building you're dealing with. On projects of this scale, the same sort of processes, pitfalls and considerations will generally apply to most projects. Therefore, this book is more about the *process* of developing more complex projects - and building your career as a developer - rather than how to develop specific types of buildings.

PRO TIP

Remember, whatever type of building you're working with, your goal is to always add value. Ultimately, it doesn't matter whether you're converting an office block, developing an existing residential building, or building something from scratch. You're adding value either by physically improving the site (which may include building on an empty plot of land) or changing the use of the building to something more valuable.

UNDERSTANDING THE RISKS

Property development is an investment - an investment of your time and money. And as with any sort of investment, there are always risks. There is risk involved even when you buy a house cheap, do it up quickly and sell it on for a profit. The market could shift. You may uncover an expensive problem that you haven't budgeted for. Your personal circumstances could unexpectedly change . . .

As you scale up your property portfolio and take on more complex projects, the risks intensify. For one thing, problems and mistakes get more costly. It's also more likely that you'll have to negotiate the planning process, which can be a significant risk in itself. And even a slight delay can be very costly if you're servicing an expensive bridge loan or development loan (see Chapter 4 for more on financing).

You know this, of course. You're not going into this with your eyes closed and fingers in your ears, chanting 'la, la, la, everything will be fine'. (Or at least, I hope you're not.)

But it's worth emphasising that, as your projects scale up, so too does your level of risk. The good news is there are many ways you can reduce your risk at various stages of your project, and these are covered in this book.

For me, the rewards far outweigh the risks, even as the size of my develop-ment projects has increased. *Especially* since the size of my development projects has increased. By scaling up my development projects – and by incorporating other property strategies that deliver a long-term income alongside capital gains – I've been able to build a successful, long-lasting career in property. I'm excited to help you do the same.

CHAPTER 2

DEVELOPING FOR PARTICULAR STRATEGIES

Many people think a successful development project starts by finding a cracking property or plot of land to develop. In fact, the work starts before then. Because, if you think about it, you can't source the right kinds of property (or land for that matter) until you've decided on your end goal. Therefore, the first step for any professional developer is to clarify your exit strategy - or, to put it another way, what successful conclusion are you looking for?

There are a couple of layers to this. Firstly, what do you intend to do with your development at the end of the project - are you planning to sell it or keep it as an investment and rent it out? This is your overarching exit strategy. Secondly, whether you're selling or renting the finished product, who are you developing for? Your target audience forms your sub-strategy and, as we'll see in this chapter, there are several sub-strategies that you can deploy as a developer. You'll also need to think about how you'll get maximum value from your chosen strategy and sub-strategy. All this is covered in this chapter.

I always have an exit strategy (and sub-strategy) in mind before I commit to a project and you should do the same. These decisions affect so much over the course of a project, not least the internal layout and overall finish.

Let's dive in and look at your overarching exit strategy.

ARE YOU BUILDING TO SELL OR RENT?

Your two main exit options are selling the property outright to generate capital growth, or renting it out to generate a longer-term income. On most (not all) of my developments, I choose the latter, but there are pros and cons to both approaches.

There's a simple reason why you need to decide this up front: your end goal informs your chosen finish. Developments that are intended for resale are generally built to a higher finish than those that are destined for the rental market. It may not be a *huge* difference in spec (I'm certainly not advocating building low-quality housing for renters), but there is nonetheless a difference.

The build-to-sell model

The biggest plus point with this exit strategy is that by selling your finished product, you earn short-term capital gains, and you can use this profit to fund future projects. However, some of the downsides include:

- Building to sell is highly dependent on the property market at the time of selling. In uncertain times, this can be a risky approach, which is why a lot of developers went bust after the 2007/2008 financial crisis. Building to rent can be considered a more stable business, and that's why I prefer it.

- The build-to-sell model is also, for me at least, more of an energy-intensive business. You're only ever as good as your last deal, and that can get exhausting after a while.

- When you sell the property (or properties), you may be liable to pay tax and National Insurance contributions on your profit if you're treated by HMRC as a trading business. Failing that, Capitals Gains Tax may be 'crystalised' (i.e. triggered). Either way, you can end up paying a lot of tax on your profit.

PRO TIP

Always talk to an accountant or tax adviser about the tax implications of selling a property versus renting it out.

The build-to-rent model

I've noticed that this approach has become much more popular with developers in recent years, with lots of developers building blocks of flats and choosing to rent out the units rather than sell them.

Obviously, the biggest downside of this model is that you don't get to sell up and collect your profit. You'll need to refinance the development in order to raise capital for future projects.

A key factor in a build-to-rent approach is the ability to add enough value in the development phase so that, when you refinance at the end of the project, you're able to withdraw most or all of the capital you initially invested. This is what enables you to do future deals. Without this additional value, you'll quickly run out of capital to fund your future investments. There's more on adding maximum value at the end of this chapter.

On the plus side, the build-to-rent model offers some significant advantages, including:

- You earn a regular income that's less prone to fluctuations in the property market. (Read more about protecting yourself against market swings and uncertainty in Chapter 10.) For me, earning a steady income from property was a critical step in becoming a full-time property investor, as opposed to someone who dabbles in it.
- Tax isn't due on the end value of the property, but on the income you earn from it. This means you've increased your equity (by adding value to the site), and this equity isn't eroded by tax.
- Assuming you intend to hold the property for at least a few years, it's likely to go up in value over time, meaning your debt is eroding and your equity is increasing as the property goes up in value.
- This coupled with rents going up over time means you can often earn significantly more profit (albeit over a longer term) with a build-to-rent model versus a resale model.

PRO TIP

One approach that I've used successfully is to develop a larger property into a block of flats designed for a rental audience, then rent out the units to tenants. I've then sold the entire block as a tenanted investment to a buyer looking for an up-and-running income stream. (I give a specific example of this in Chapter 9.) Technically, this would still fall under the build-to-rent approach, since you're building for a rental audience, not a resale audience, but it shows that the right build-to-rent development can still deliver capital gains, if that's what you want.

WHICH MODEL IS RIGHT FOR YOU?

It should be clear by now that I mostly favour the build-to-rent model, but, ultimately, there's no right or wrong exit option. The key is to pick the right model for you at this stage in your development career. When weighing up your options, be guided by factors such as:

- Your local housing market. Local demographics will play an important role here, as one model may be much more suited to your local area. You can always talk to some agents to get a feel for how the local sales and rental markets are doing.
- Your available capital. This applies to your target audience as well as overarching exit strategy, but let me mention it here. At the end of the day, you may not be able to afford to develop luxury apartments in a desirable town centre location at this stage in your career. You might be better off on the fringes of town, where you can do a more cost-effective development. And this more affordable location may impact your target audience and whether you build to sell or rent.
- Your passion and experience. If you're passionate about sales and you get a kick out of the 'only as good as your last deal' mindset,

then build-to-sell is probably more up your street. The daily grind of owning and renting properties isn't for everyone (although, you can always cut down your workload as a landlord by employing a lettings agent – see Chapter 9). Or maybe you've got experience as a buy-to-let landlord, or have run a little holiday let in the past, in which case that may stand you in good stead for a build-to-rent approach.

- Your personal goals. For example, if you really want to retire early and earn a passive income, then building to rent is probably a better model for you.
- Your risk profile. I feel that building to sell is a higher-risk model, unless you're a huge developer who does so many sites you can balance the risk. If you're working one or two sites a year, which is likely at this stage in your career, building to sell comes with more risk. Personally, I see building to rent as giving me more control.

PRO TIP

A sensible approach that I favour is to build to rent, but build it *well*, with a slightly above average spec compared to other rental properties. This means if I do decide to sell at the end of the build, the quality will be (just about) good enough for a resale market. (Obviously this doesn't apply if you're targeting very high-end buyers.) You have to be prepared to invest in a slightly higher-quality spec than most rentals, but it can be worth it to give yourself multiple exit options. I talk more about multiple exit options later in the chapter.

DECIDING YOUR SUB-STRATEGY

Largely this means deciding who you're building for. But you may also decide to specialise in certain types of development. Let's look at both.

Becoming an expert in certain types of development

By specialising in a particular type of development, you get better at it every time, it becomes easier to source suitable buildings, your development costs come down, and you build a strong reputation as an expert developer in that field.

PRO TIP

Consider specialising in an approach that's easily replicable – something you can do time and time again, and become an expert in.

As an example, I do a lot of commercial-to-residential conversions, converting offices, care homes and hotels into apartment blocks. These sorts of properties lend themselves really well to residential conversions, and my end product could potentially be anything from one- and two-bedroom apartments right down to studios and micro-studios, depending on the specific location and target audience. In fact, in my area, there's a lot of demand among young professionals for studios and micro-studios, so I've been building more of these in recent years.

That doesn't mean I'm not open to other types of development. I am. But I've definitely found that specialising in particular types of developments has boosted my career. I've grown in confidence and have quickly become an expert in producing high-quality conversions. As a bonus, I've built a reputation in my area for doing these types of builds, which sometimes means potential sites come my way more easily; for example, an agent might call me up before a commercial building hits the open market because she knows it's just the sort of thing I specialise in. (Read more about sourcing sites in Chapter 5.)

Deciding who you want to sell or rent to

Regardless of whether you're building to sell or building to rent, you need to have a good idea of your target audience. So, on a build-to-sell model, are you targeting first-time buyers, young families, executive home buyers, luxury buyers, retirement buyers, or a different audience altogether?

PRO TIP

If you aren't sure which target audience is right for you, talk to a handful of local estate agents or lettings agents to get a feel for the biggest target market in the local area.

Similarly, with a build-to-rent model, there are different renters you can target, such as:

- Professionals (which could mean a family, a couple, a single tenant, or friends living together)
- Low income or social housing tenants
- Students
- Short-term renters (such as professionals renting serviced accommodation while they're in town for contract work or tourists renting a holiday let)

Your target audience – whether renters or buyers – will inform everything about your development, from the type of property you source (and its location) to the end finish. Fixtures, fittings, appliances, décor, even the layout . . . it all depends on your target audience.

PRO TIP

Once you've decided on a target audience, you should do your homework and create a clear picture of what that audience expects or needs from a property.

Good questions to ask include:

- What's the best location for your audience?
- What sort of sale or rental price can you expect in that location?
- How big does a property have to be to satisfy your target audience? How many bedrooms, bathrooms and reception rooms will your audience expect/need?
- How big will those rooms need to be? While you might need a large kitchen for the luxury family market, that's really not necessary for students.
- Will your target audience expect or need any kind of outdoor space, whether it's a large garden or a small balcony? An easy-to-maintain patio garden might be ideal for a professional house share setup, but won't work for buyers looking for a family home.

At this stage, you should be looking to build a thorough understanding of your audience's needs before you start looking for development opportunities (see Chapter 5 for more on sourcing developments).

Understanding that there are multiple different rental strategies

You'll have gathered by now that build-to-rent can actually feed into a number of different rental sub-strategies. I realised early in my property career that there were many different strategies for earning money from rental properties, beyond the obvious single let route (where you rent a whole flat or house on a long-term lease). I much prefer to focus on those rental strategies that offer maximum return on my investment.

PRO TIP

Multi-tenant strategies or short-term leases can significantly increase your returns and boost the value of your development.

Good rental strategies to consider include:

- Houses in multiple occupation (HMOs). My first step into property investing came when I turned my then house into an HMO and rented out the spare rooms to different tenants. Therefore, an HMO is a property (house or flat) that is rented out on a room-by-room basis, rather than rented out as a whole. This is a popular approach among renters because renting a room in a house or flat is far more affordable than renting a whole home. And landlords love it because you can make far more money and reduce your risk of void periods (where the property sits empty) - particularly if you develop whole blocks of flats for HMO use, as I often do. I highly recommended this booming strategy.
- Renting to students and social housing tenants. I get that this isn't something that immediately appeals to many landlords, but there's good income to be made from renting to students and low-income

tenants. In certain locations (such as a university town or an economically depressed area), this approach can make much more sense than renting to professionals.

- Serviced accommodation. This rental strategy involves renting out properties (often apartments) on a short-term basis. It's a highly scalable approach that can cover anything from single Airbnb apartments to whole aparthotels. I've successfully developed an aparthotel that was subsequently rented to professionals who were in the area on short-term work contracts.
- Holiday lets. This is a strategy that appeals to many people. And depending on your location, it can be incredibly lucrative.
- Lease options. I mention this purely as a low-capital alternative to buying and developing a property. With a lease option, you rent out a property and then (with permission) sublet it to tenants. Crucially, the lease option gives you the opportunity to buy the property in future.

I'm really passionate about educating investors and developers on the range of different property strategies out there. So much so that I've written a whole book on the subject. Check out *Professional Property Investment Strategies* if you'd like to read more about these and other property strategies. You can also turn to chapter 10 to learn about the importance of diversifying your property portfolio through multiple strategies.

GIVING YOURSELF MORE THAN ONE EXIT OPTION

I don't want to contradict myself here, but sometimes it pays to have a backup plan.

To be clear, you absolutely should pick a firm exit strategy and target audience, and work to achieve your intended outcome. However, particularly when you're building to sell, it's a good idea to keep a 'plan B' in mind. In other words, what will you do if you can't sell your development because the market has changed? Having a backup plan helps to reduce your risk and gives you a safety net, should you need it.

This may even apply on build-to-rent projects. Say, for example, you're developing with professional tenants in mind but something happens to depress the local rental market. Or maybe you're developing serviced accommodation or holiday lets and, for whatever reason, people stop travelling to your area. (Big changes in the rental market are rare but, as COVID-19 demonstrated, to the horror of many Airbnb operators, it can happen.) Will you pivot to a different rental audience or try to sell the property?

I generally prefer to develop properties to a fairly high specification, with quality kitchens, bathrooms, etc. This does mean my development costs are a little higher, but I've found it's worth the extra spend to reduce my risk and give me more leeway at the end of the project. For example, a quality resale property will always attract good tenants if I can't sell. Likewise, a higher-spec rental property should still be attractive to buyers in the event that I need to sell. Or I could, at a push, put lower-income tenants in the property.

PRO TIP

Remember, you can't attract higher-quality tenants or buyers to a property that has been developed with a lower-spec audience in mind. So think carefully about your finish and go for the best quality you can reasonably afford.

Read more tips for reducing your risk in Chapter 10.

DEVELOPING FOR MAXIMUM VALUE

Your overarching exit strategy and sub-strategy plays a big role in how much value you can squeeze from your developments. For example, some rental strategies, such as an HMO strategy, will earn you much more rental income than a straightforward single let.

If you're planning to hold onto the building, you will also need to think about how long you intend to own it for. Holding a building for 20 years is very different to holding it for five years in terms of the amount of profit you can accumulate. This may inform how much value you need to add to the development.

But one of the biggest factors in developing for maximum value is using the internal layout wisely so that you can create as much rental or saleable space as possible. Let's delve into this in a little more detail.

Getting more gross development value (GDV) out of your projects

I talk more about GDV (i.e. the amount a site will be worth after development) in Chapter 5, but for now I want to emphasise the importance of maximising your GDV. Whatever your exit strategy – selling or renting – you want as much GDV from your projects as possible.

Layout is one of the best ways to achieve this – specifically, designing the layout so that you're creating additional rental or saleable space. As an example, when I convert commercial buildings into flats, I might achieve maximum value by:

- Minimising the number of corridors and size of communal areas to create extra space for flats.
- Demolishing extra stairwells or entrances to create additional living space in the building.

- Demolishing chimneys and fireplaces to gain extra space within rooms.
- Building up into the ceiling space by adding mezzanines. The great thing about developing office buildings is they often have nice high ceilings to take advantage of.
- Converting a basement into living space.
- Designing a layout that allows for the flats to be used as HMOs, as well as straightforward single lets. For instance, clever use of an extra internal door on a flat's master bathroom, means it could be used as an en-suite for a bedroom. Check out the case study at the end of this chapter for an example of this in action.

As much as possible, you want to 'sweat the asset!', which in terms of property means getting as much usable space out of a building as possible. Obviously, you'll need to work closely with a good architect to achieve this. More on that coming up.

PRO TIP

Sometimes a building or plot might be offered for sale with planning permission. In these cases, more often than not, the seller recognises that they'll get more for their site with planning permission, so they get an architect to knock up some basic plans – just enough to get permission. However, because the seller isn't approaching the design from a developer's mindset, meaning they're not thinking about GDV, there could be an opportunity for you to add yet more value, meaning you amend the design to increase the GDV and resubmit for planning consent. You could even potentially sell the site at a tidy profit on the basis of this higher-value design, without even having to build the development yourself.

Working with your architect to extract as much value as possible from the design

All this obviously feeds into the brief you give your architect. In my experience, architects have a brilliant eye for design, but aren't necessarily great at understanding the commercial aspects of what you're trying to achieve. So it's up to you to explain your vision and be crystal clear on how you want to extract maximum value from the design.

PRO TIP

The architect is there to implement your vision for your end product, not decide that vision for you. I think of it like this: the architect is there to enhance the aesthetics and ensure good design, but it's my responsibility to ensure the design is right for my strategy, and that it delivers maximum value.

In practice, this means you'll need to be pretty specific with your architect. I talk more about the design stage in Chapter 7, but as a quick example, let's say I'm converting an office block into flats. Before I talk to the architect, I'll already have a good idea of how many flats I can expect to create per floor (based on the total size of the building and the current minimum space requirement for new homes). I'll then get the architect to do me a design based on this.

With the growing popularity of micro-studios (which are defined as any property smaller than the current minimum space requirement of 37 sqm), good space design is more important than ever. Whenever you're building smaller units, keep in mind that it's not just about squeezing as many units as possible into a building. You need to give your buyers or tenants a feeling of space - for example, by creating additional mezzanine space, maximising light and adding built-in storage. And it's really important to create a feeling of quality through the fixtures and fittings. This is all part of adding maximum value in a small space.

As well as working with your architect to achieve a good design, you may need to involve other professionals at this stage, such as:

- Quantity surveyor, to get costings for different design ideas
- Planning consultant, to see what's feasible in terms of planning
- Approved building control inspector, to check that the design is legal from a building regulations point of view

In other words, it's all very well coming up with a clever design, but it has to work financially and from the building control and planning perspectives. Turn to Chapter 3 to read more about the 'dream team' of professionals you'll need to work with on your developments.

CASE STUDY: GETTING MAXIMUM VALUE FROM A LAYOUT

The project

Conversion of a building into flats, using layout and additional internal doors to maximise usability.

The details

I wanted to use this case study to show how even a simple design trick can add extra value to a rental property. In this case, an additional internal door added value by ensuring a straightforward apartment layout would also work as an HMO flat, thereby generating a higher rental income.

The key takeaway

Don't underestimate the impact design and layout can have on your GDV. Make sure you fully explain your goals to your architect so they can turn that vision into a workable design.

CHAPTER 3

BUILDING YOUR DEVELOPMENT DREAM TEAM

Power team, dream team, whatever you want to call it, these are the professionals you need to work with when successfully taking a development project from start to finish. If I tried to do even half the jobs required on the average development myself, it would take forever and the quality would be, well, not great. I simply don't have the right training or skills. But more importantly, it's not how I want to spend my time.

This is why you need a dream team.

Part of the reason I wanted to write this book was to give growing developers a better understanding of how to work with the various experts involved in the property development lifecycle - including who you need, how to find people you can trust, and how to get the most out of your dream team. For me, having a great dream team is a critical driver of success, which is why I've dedicated an entire chapter to the topic.

REMEMBER, YOU NEED TO TREAT YOUR DEVELOPMENT PORTFOLIO AS A BUSINESS

If you want to become a full-time property developer and earn a comfortable income, you need to start thinking of your development portfolio as a business – and yourself as a business owner. And one of the key lessons any business owner learns is that you need to be working *on* your business not *in* your business. In practical terms, this means working on growing your business and achieving your business goals, rather than handling the day-to-day minutia that keeps your business (in this case, your developments) ticking along.

It's really important you use your time wisely as a developer. If you try to do too many tasks yourself (i.e. working *in* your business) your developments will take longer, it will be far more stressful, and the end result may not be as good as it could be – which will negatively impact your GDV (see Chapter 2). Far better to spend your time growing your business by sourcing new sites, expanding your network, connecting with potential investors, and learning how best to leverage different forms of funding (see Chapter 4) and maybe even different property strategies (see Chapter 10). These are all things that will help you take your development career to the next level.

I'd give the same advice to any growing developer, regardless of their skill level. Even if you're a master builder, you still need to be working *on* your business, not in it.

PRO TIP

Doing things yourself – project managing being a prime example – seems like a cost saving on the surface. But it can lead to expensive delays and mistakes. Far better to spend the money and have your developments running smoothly. Plus, although it may seem counterintuitive, engaging the right professionals at the right stage of your developments can save you far more money in the long run. Your projects will be less prone to going over budget and over time.

Expert help can also help you add even more value to your developments. As an example, I might work with a specialist fire consultant at the design stage. This may seem like an unnecessary expense, but if the fire consultant confirms that I can demolish an extra internal staircase to make way for more sellable or rentable space, while still complying with fire safety regs, that means I can squeeze more value out of the building and increase my profit. It's therefore money well spent. The same can be said of the many consultants I regularly use to assess sites and provide design reports.

PRO TIP

Instead of focusing on how much it costs to employ specialists, try to think of it in terms of the value they add to your business.

Ultimately, as your business grows, so too will the number of consultants, freelancers and experts you need to rely on to successfully complete developments. In part, this will be because you need to outsource more tasks. But it's also a natural part of taking on more complex projects.

SO, WHO MIGHT YOU NEED IN YOUR DEVELOPMENT DREAM TEAM?

When I first sat down to write this chapter, I had planned to organise the full list of my dream team members according to the typical stages of a development. But it soon become obvious that there's just too much overlap between the stages. For instance, the project management company that I work with might get involved when I'm first assessing a potential new site, as well as during the pre-construction and construction stages. Similarly, I might engage a quantity surveyor to assess the costs of developing a site, not just during the build itself.

Therefore, it makes sense to think of the development dream team in terms of:

- The core team – these are the professionals I work with all the time, right from the start of a development project. These people help me do my early due diligence, find and assess good sites, and complete purchases.
- Main site team – spanning design and build, these are the pre-construction and construction professionals that I engage on pretty much every build.
- Project-specific site team – these are the consultants that I may or may not need on specific projects, depending on the site's unique requirements.
- Post-completion team – these professionals help me sell my developed properties or manage buildings on an ongoing basis (where I'm retaining them for rental income).

I've tried to be as thorough as possible here, based on my previous developments. Obviously, your own developments will be different, and you may not need all of these professionals on all of your projects. So don't be scared by these lists! And if you want to see me talk more about my own development dream team, check out my YouTube channel.

In many cases, your project manager will advise you on which professionals you do and don't need to hire.

Let's get into the lists . . .

Core team

- Project manager – I consider my project manager to be one of the most important people I work with. They help me assess potential sites, engage various consultants, liaise with the architect, appoint contractors, and much, much more. For more reasons not to project manage your own builds, turn to Chapter 7.
- Commercial mortgage broker/independent financial adviser – you don't want a regular residential mortgage broker here. You want someone who can help you take advantage of the more advanced finance options designed for developers.
- Accountant and tax adviser – there are lots of tax implications around selling or renting your developments, so be sure to work with an accountant or tax adviser to manage your finances as efficiently as possible.
- Property solicitor – to coordinate the legal aspects of transactions. You may also need specialist agreements drawn up over time, such as tenancy agreements or joint venture agreements with investors.
- Estate agents or property sourcing agents – although I often source sites myself, I still cultivate good relationships with local agents and specialist deal sourcers (see Chapter 5).
- Insurance broker – it's vital you work with a good independent insurance broker to ensure your projects are properly covered according to the project stage.

- Planning consultant – an essential resource, my planning consultant will advise on planning implications and manage the planning application process for me (see Chapter 6).
- Quantity surveyor – a good QS will save you money over the course of your projects by weighing up the costs of different design options, fixtures, fittings, etc. and then helping to manage costs during the build. I'll often involve my QS as soon as I make an offer on a site, so that I can accurately estimate the build costs.
- Architect – I prefer to engage a separate architect to draw up the floorplans and detailed design drawings, rather than hire a contractor on a 'design and build' basis. Read more about this in Chapter 7.

Main site team

- Building surveyor – before buying a site, I'd appoint a surveyor to carry out an in-depth structural survey of the building. This is different to the lender's valuation survey, which is purely about assessing the value of the site, not its integrity.
- M&E (mechanical and electrical) engineer – this encompasses all the building's mechanical and electrical systems, and may include things like heating, cooling, lighting, ventilation, pipework, electrical systems, elevators, environmental design and renewable energy systems. M&E forms a critical part of any design, and may add up to a big chunk of your development budget.
- Fire engineer – to help identify the risks and design safeguards that will protect your building against fire, control the effects of fire, and safeguard the occupants.
- Approved inspector/building control inspector – the person that will help you obtain building regulation approval. While you can simply work with your local authority's building control department, I actually prefer to use an independent, third-party approved inspector. In my experience, independent inspectors are more

commercially minded and pragmatic, and will help to overcome problems more easily. They'll also handle the official building control signoff and certification.

- Acoustic consultant – when you're converting buildings from one use to another, it's really important to consider the acoustic impacts on the eventual occupants. You may, for example, need to pay out for acoustic flooring. Funnily enough I originally trained as an acoustic engineer, so this is one area where I do have the knowledge and skills to do it myself, but I still pay experts to come in and do acoustic tests on my sites.
- Asbestos surveyor – unless you're dealing with industrial buildings, you're unlikely to encounter major asbestos problems these days. However, lenders often require an asbestos assessment, which is why I've included this in with the main site team.
- Contract administrator or employer's agent – this role kicks in at the stage of hiring the contractor, to ensure the project progresses according to the contract. This person may or may not be the same as your project manager. I talk more about this in Chapter 7.
- Building contractor (who will in turn appoint various tradespeople) – on most projects, you'll probably seek tenders from multiple different building contractors before deciding which one you want to work with. Over time, though, you'll likely end up with a few favourite contractors that you work with more than others. Read more about the construction process in Chapter 8.

Project-specific site team

- Façade/cladding and windows consultants – while this is important from the design and building performance perspectives, it may not be essential on every site.
- Structural/civil engineer – different to the building surveyor, this service may be required if you're doing major structural work to a building.

- Drainage engineer – particularly important when you're repurposing a building for another use, you need to ensure the drainage system can cope with the intended use.
- Ground sub-scan surveyor – if, for example, you need to dig new trenches for drainage, you want to know what's under your building. This may also be needed for the groundworks stage of new-build projects.
- Arboriculture consultant – if your development needs to be tree-friendly or work around important trees, this is the expert you need. In fact, this may be a requirement of securing planning permission.
- Bat surveyor – again, this may be a requirement for planning.
- Topographical surveyor – needed to determine any land-specific challenges, for example, where you may need to level off ground.
- Contamination consultant – another one that's often, but not always, needed for planning permission, this expert will assess the risk of contamination to future occupants of the building.
- Highways consultant – your local authority may require a highways report to assess the impact of your development on local roads and traffic.
- Party wall surveyor – there to resolve disputes with neighbours in relation to party walls, boundaries and excavations that take place near neighbouring buildings.
- Rights of light surveyor – which may be needed to determine whether your proposed development infringes on a neighbour's enjoyment of natural light.
- IT/broadband consultant – to assess any challenges with getting broadband services to the property.

This is a long list, but it's in no way exhaustive. Specific projects may throw up specific challenges that aren't featured on this list. For example, you may need a flooding consultant, environmental impact consultant, archaeologist, lighting designer, structural waterproofing consultant or any number of other experts that you've never heard of!

Over time, you'll get to know which consultants are needed on which types of projects. However, your project manager will also be able to help with this, as will your planning consultant (in terms of which assessments might be necessary to satisfy the planners).

Post-completion team

- Estate agent - when selling your finished product, you may not work with the same sort of agent who helped you source the development in the first place. For example, you might want to partner with an agent who specialises in marketing properties to investor buyers. Read more about this in Chapter 9.
- Lettings agent/property manager - if you're renting out the property, a lettings agent or property manager can take care of finding tenants and managing the property on your behalf (including repairs and maintenance). Again, there's more on this in Chapter 9.

PRO TIP

I hope these lists demonstrate just how much work goes into more complex developments – and highlights some of the areas where you perhaps didn't know you needed specialist advice. (As the saying goes, you don't know what you don't know. Well, now you know!) Bottom line, it's not just a case of finding a good local builder. You need a broad range of consultants on board to ensure your sites get developed properly.

HOW TO FIND AND VET PEOPLE FOR YOUR CORE TEAM

I have, over the years, built up connections with a large team of experts that I can call upon, depending on each project's requirements. But what if you don't have these sorts of connections? Where on earth do you start?

Well, for the main site team and project-specific site team, your project manager will help you appoint the right experts, based on the site's specific requirements. Sometimes your choice of consultant will come down to your budget and availability of consultants, but you should also consider whether they have worked on that type of site before. It's no good hiring a drainage consultant with no experience of residential properties when that's precisely what you're building.

For the core team - including your project manager - it's generally up to you to find the right people. So how can you find good people, and make sure they're up to the task? My top tips are:

- It's really important your core team is made up of people you can trust so always start with word-of-mouth recommendations from people you know. Ask your friends, colleagues and acquaintances if they've worked with a good property solicitor, project manager, accountant, and so on.
- You can also search online, or look on property forums and communities, such as wealthlabs.co.uk. But whenever you're searching for experts that haven't come via a word-of-mouth recommendation, always do your due diligence and check out their reviews.
- Search via the relevant accrediting bodies. For example, a quantity surveyor should be accredited through RICS, the Royal Institution of Chartered Surveyors. Again, you should still do your due diligence here.
- Go to property-specific networking meetings and national shows to expand your network and connect with useful contacts.

- A mentor may also be able to connect you with core team members. For example, when I mentor property developers, I connect them with my preferred project management firm, funders, and so on. Read more about mentorship in Chapter 11.
- Meet face-to-face with potential core team members at least once to gauge how well you might work with them.
- Assess their experience, skill level and liability insurance. It's really important they have a proven track record on your type of developments and, just as important, that they're insured to take on your types of projects.
- Ask to speak to one or two of their clients for a reference. For someone like a project manager, you should also be able to visit previous sites that they've managed.
- Ask yourself, do I like this person? Can I see myself enjoying working with them? If the answer is no, even if they're highly skilled, you may be better off continuing the search. After all, in an ideal scenario, your core team will be working with you on every development for many years to come.
- Ask yourself, does it seem like they want my business? What I mean by this is do they respond to your initial emails quickly? Do they pick up the phone when you call? If you have to work hard to get someone's attention, it doesn't bode well.

KEEPING YOUR DREAM TEAM HAPPY

Once you've found good people, it's really important to keep them on your side.

Here are my top recommendations for keeping your dream team happy, engaged and keen to continue working with you.

- Hopefully it goes without saying that you should always pay people on time.
- Keep in touch regularly. Not only does this ensure your projects run more smoothly, it also helps to build rapport. I talk to my project manager almost daily when we're collaborating on a project. And even if I'm not currently working with someone (for example, an estate agent), I might still drop them an occasional email asking how they are.
- Be very clear about your expectations. Miscommunications can wreak havoc on your projects so always agree (preferably in writing) what work you need doing, and to what standard.
- Review your arrangement regularly. Ideally you'd do this every six months, or at least once a year. This review doesn't need to be anything too formal - just a chat about how the arrangement is going and whether anything could be done to make things run more smoothly.
- Respect people's time. Don't waste people's time, or call them at 9pm, or email them when you know they're on holiday. Treat your dream team members' time as carefully as your own.
- Recommend your experts to others in your network. Providing there's no conflict of interest, why shouldn't you recommend

your amazing dream team members to other people you know? Remember, referrals work both ways, so if you're helping out your experts by recommending their business, they'll be more inclined to do the same for you. And they'll probably be far more connected in the construction industry than you . . .

- Give credit where credit's due. Everyone likes to hear that they're doing a good job, so say thank you for a job well done and express how much you appreciate your team's support.

Follow these tips, build a good relationship with your dream team members and, take it from me, you'll be making your life as a successful developer so much easier.

CHAPTER 4

HOW TO FUND YOUR DEVELOPMENT PROJECTS

When you first start out in property development, you may be funding your projects through a standard residential mortgage, savings or personal borrowings. But as your projects scale up in complexity and budget, those routes are probably no longer an option. Instead, you'll need to tap into more specialised funding.

Strictly speaking, you would source a potential development property and estimate the development costs before you seek out finance, so you might be wondering why I'm covering finance now, before the chapter on sourcing properties. It's because, in my experience, finance can make the difference between someone who develops properties as an on-the-side gig and someone who is able to turn it into a full-time career.

PRO TIP

Being aware of the different funding options – and being willing to sometimes take a more creative approach to financing – is, in my opinion, a critical part of success. It can give you an edge over other, less savvy property developers. I'd go so far as to say it's easily as important as choosing the right end strategy (see Chapter 2) and sourcing the right property (Chapter 5).

Here, I walk you through the main funding considerations that apply to larger developments. I'm assuming that a traditional mortgage, buy-to-let mortgage or end refinance loan isn't an option, which means you'll likely have to seek out one of the following options:

- Bridging loan
- Land and development loan
- Creative finance opportunities, such as joint venture partnerships or private lending

But before we get into these options, let's talk a bit about property valuation.

UNDERSTANDING PROPERTY VALUATION METHODS – AND WHY THEY MATTER TO YOUR DEVELOPMENTS

You probably already have a decent grasp of the standard market comparison approach to valuation (as in, working out how much a property is worth, or could be worth, based on comparable properties in the same area). You'll also know that understanding valuation is key to ensuring you don't pay too much for a property and, later, being able to achieve the right sale price after you've developed it.

However, working out the end value of a project (and, ultimately, your gross development value (GDV)) does get more complex as you take on slightly bigger or trickier developments. What's more, valuation affects the amount you can borrow to buy and develop a site. Which is why I wanted to cover valuation before talking about the different types of funding.

Calculating GDV is about more than just working out how much a property will be worth. To work out whether a project is financially viable, you must also take into account how much it costs to buy and develop the site. You can read more about sourcing and assessing suitable development opportunities (including financial viability) in Chapter 5. For now, let's focus on how properties are valued.

A few valuation basics

Let's start with a brief definition of valuation, which may or may not be obvious:

- Valuation is the process of determining what a property is actually *worth*.
- A property's value may not be the same as its actual *price*. In fact, there are a number of occasions where you might pay less than a property is worth (such as a distressed sale) or potentially pay more than it's currently worth (to secure a particularly attractive site, for example).

PRO TIP

No doubt a professional surveyor or appraiser will be involved in every property deal you make - usually appointed by the lender to ensure the property is worth their investment. However, it's still important to understand how surveyors arrive at valuations. Knowing how surveyors calculate a property's value has helped me work out exactly what I should be paying for sites, and find the right sort of funding for that value.

Plus, because I know what the surveyor is looking at, I've often been able to give supporting evidence to help achieve a more accurate valuation, or to ensure the valuation isn't overly conservative (which, again, is useful when you're after a certain amount of funding from a lender).

The two main types of valuation methods that are relevant to property developers are:

- Market comparison approach
- Investment or income value approach

One approach isn't necessarily better than the other as such; it's just that they will each be more appropriate for different situations.

Let's look at each area in turn.

Market comparison valuations

Also known as the 'bricks and mortar' or 'comparable' approach, you'll already be familiar with this approach because it's how estate agents value your house when you put it up for sale. Basically, with this method, the property being valued is compared with other similar properties in the same location that have recently been sold.

This method works really well on standard residential properties, but when you get to commercial properties or large, unusual residential properties, finding suitable comparisons can be a challenge. In cases like this, the market comparison method isn't always the best judge of value. Which brings us to . . .

The investment or income value approach

This method considers the income a property is already generating or could potentially generate through rental income, which means it's commonly used for commercial properties or income-producing residential properties (such as HMOs or blocks of flats). This is a really useful method for growing property developers to get to grips with.

To value a property using the investment value approach, the surveyor will:

- Start by calculating the *gross* annual rental income generated by the property (which could also include income from renting out parking spaces).
- Then they work out the *net* annual rental income by applying a deduction to the gross income (this deduction takes account of things like void periods and maintenance fees). Typically, the deduction is between 15% and 25%, but it depends on factors such as the strength of the local rental market, location and quality of the property.

- And finally, they will divide the net income by the typical *yield* for that type of property in that area. (Yield being return on investment expressed as a percentage. In my part of the country, yield will typically range between 6% and 7.5% but, again, this will vary in different locations.) This gives you the *end value*.

PRO TIP

If you want to use this approach yourself to estimate the value of a property, you can always chat to local surveyors about what sort of yield is currently being applied to similar properties in the same area.

When weighing up potential development opportunities, try doing a 'back of the envelope' contrast between the market comparison and investment value approaches. You could be surprised at the difference.

As a simple example, if you take a large house that's currently being marketed as a standard residential property, the market comparison approach might value the property at £500,000. However, if you were planning to turn that property into an eight bedroom HMO – where each of the bedrooms are rented out separately, thereby generating significant rental income – then the investment valuation approach might value the property at £750,000. I've literally had differences in valuations as large as this (and more), precisely because the surveyors were using different approaches.

As you can imagine, this can have a huge impact on the amount you can borrow to buy and develop a site. What's more, should you choose to retain a property you've developed, and refinance it, then the valuation method used will impact how much you can refinance the property for. And if you can achieve a higher valuation, you have more flexibility to leverage the property for future investments.

Working with the surveyor and lender to achieve the valuation you want

The good news is, there are steps you can take to achieve a more positive valuation and secure the amount of funding you need.

How this might work in practice is:

- You ask to join the surveyor on the day of the valuation – you could do this even when the surveyor has been appointed by the lender. (See below if this isn't a possibility.)
- You research other properties in the area (rental income, yield, etc.) and do your own calculations on what the property might be worth in advance of the lender's valuation.

- You then offer to share your research with the surveyor. You can do this in person on the day of the valuation, or reach out to the lender in advance of the inspection if it's not possible to meet the surveyor in person. (In my experience, so long as you don't act like you know how to do the surveyor's job better than them, most are happy to receive your supporting evidence.)
- If you're not satisfied with the valuation given, you can always get a second opinion from an independent surveyor - based on their valuation, you could potentially make your case directly to the lender. And if all else fails, you may decide to seek funding elsewhere.

TAPPING INTO BRIDGING LOANS

Also known as refurbishment finance, a bridging loan is a specialist loan that can be used either to fund the development of a property, or ideally to cover the costs of purchasing the property *and* the development costs. Bridging loans are available to cover 'light' refurbishments and 'heavy' refurbishments - meaning different lenders offer different products. There's no point presenting your development project to a lender if they only allow minimal, light refurbishments and your development doesn't fit that bill.

PRO TIP

It's vital you work with an independent broker to determine which funding route is best for you – and that applies whether you're going for a bridging loan or development loan (more on that coming up later). You can get help finding a broker on our free wealth-building platform, wealthlabsco.uk, where you can read more about different finance options and talk to our recommended specialists.

What makes bridging loans useful to developers?

- As the name suggests, bridging finance is designed to help you 'bridge' a financial gap and, as such, can be arranged at short notice and with less information than other types of financing. So if you need to move fast on a deal, a bridging loan can help you get there.
- They're interest-only, and rather than make monthly repayments, you pay back the entire loan amount at the end of the loan term (or, ideally, sooner).
- Many lenders will offer a loan-to-value (LTV) of up to 75% of the property's value (some will even base this on the GDV, or post-development value of the property). Under certain circumstances, you may even be able to secure a higher LTV.
- You can secure lending against properties that other lenders won't lend against, such as a very rundown or uninhabitable property.

So when would you go for a bridging loan? Generally speaking, bridging loans are intended to be short-term loans only, often to be repaid within one year or less. So I'd say bridging loans are really only an option on sites where the development schedule is pretty short, and the development costs are relatively small compared to the cost of buying the property. The idea is, you fund the development out of the bridge loan, complete it quickly, then refinance to a regular mortgage or sell the property and pay back the loan.

If you're looking at a pretty lengthy or expensive development - where you won't be able to fund the costs of the development out of the bridging loan LTV - then a specialist development loan is likely to be a better bet. Your broker will be able to advise on which is best for you.

PRO TIP

As with any loan, your credit rating has a huge impact on whether you can obtain finance to develop your properties, and how favourable the terms of the loan will be. Even finding a great broker is easier when you have a good credit score. Therefore, it's vital you regularly check your credit report, using a credit check company such as Experian. (The paid-for service offered by such companies is well worth it, as you won't be limited on how often you can access your credit report.) Keep an especially close eye on your credit report in the run up to applying for funding. And if you spot any mistakes on your credit report (which does happen – it's happened to me), you'll need to talk to the creditor in question to get the mistake rectified.

SEEKING OUT DEVELOPMENT FINANCING

As you start getting into projects where the developments costs are higher – potentially edging towards or even exceeding the purchase price – it's more likely you'll need specialised development financing (i.e. a land and development loan) to fund the project.

As an example, my company bought a commercial site for £1.4 million, and then spent £1.85 million developing it into residential flats to achieve a final end value of £5 million. On projects like this – where the cost of development is high in relation to the site's current value – you probably won't be able to fund the purchase and development with a bridge loan. Whereas, subject to LTV restraints from the lender, even a large development spend can potentially be funded entirely through development financing.

PRO TIP

Don't be afraid of projects with a big development cost. After all, it's all about adding value to maximise your return on investment. Often buying a site on the cheap (I use that word loosely, given the value of some of my projects) and spending more than the purchase price on developing it can reap huge rewards.

So what is development financing? Well, unlike a bridging loan, which may or may not cover the cost of buying *and* developing a site, development financing is specifically designed to fund both stages.

As such, development finance breaks down into two portions: the 'land loan' portion and the 'development loan' portion. Which is why you'll often hear development financing referred to as land and development loans.

- The 'land loan' funds the original purchase. Don't be confused by the name - land loans can be used to buy a plot of land or an existing property, and can be used for commercial as well as residential sites. Depending on the provider, the LTV ratio on land loans can range from 50% to as much as 75% or 80%. You'll obviously need some upfront capital, then, to secure such a loan and buy the site. For developers, this generally means leveraging other properties that you own (circle back to Chapter 2 for more on build-to-rent), freeing up capital by selling previous sites, or tapping into private funding (more on this coming up).
- Having purchased the site, the 'development loan' then covers the cost of the development. By working with a good broker, you'll often be able to secure up to 100% of the cost of the development work. The development portion of the loan is usually released in instalments (drawdowns) as you complete certain phases of the build. This means you can expect the lender to monitor your progress on the

project closely, probably sending a surveyor to the site at regular intervals to value the work that's been done. If a certain milestone or valuation isn't met, the lender will typically refuse to release the next drawdown, which means it's vital you keep a tight rein on your project schedule and cash flow - I've heard too many horror stories of developments failing because the developer simply ran out of cash. (Read more about cash flow and keeping your lender happy in Chapter 8.)

You can usually get both the land and development portions from the same lender - although it may work out better for your project to source the land part from one lender and the development portion from a different lender. It all depends on your project specifics, lender terms, the current market, etc. Again, it's really important to work with a good broker here.

Note that development financing isn't cheap in terms of fees and interest rates, and you may be asked to provide evidence of your track record as a developer or provide a personal guarantee.

PRO TIP

Some lenders will expect you to provide a personal guarantee to secure the loan (that's on top of the loan being secured against the asset in question). A personal guarantee means if you default on the loan, the lender can come after your other assets to recoup their losses. (And yes, that's on top of repossessing the property!) Having to give a personal guarantee isn't necessarily a dealbreaker - I'm usually happy to do it, but I've got a lot of experience and am confident in my ability to deliver projects successfully. Just be aware of what you're agreeing to, basically. And if you are agreeing to a personal guarantee, make sure your end strategy, project costs, schedule, etc. are as watertight as possible.

One final warning note on development financing: remember that the value of a property can go down before it goes up. That commercial building I bought for £1.4 million? We then stripped it out and ripped it apart in order to start the conversion, which meant, for a brief while, it was worth less than when I bought it. By this point it was no longer usable as an office and was essentially just a shell. If your funding is released based on meeting certain valuations rather than build milestones, you'll need to keep this in mind and build a healthy contingency into your project.

DECIDING ON THE BEST FUNDING OPTION FOR YOUR PROJECT

While you can go directly to lenders to seek funding, I firmly believe a good mortgage broker is worth their weight in gold, particularly as you begin to move away from standard mortgages and into the territory of bridging loans and development finance. I *always* work with a broker to secure funding, even though I've been doing this for years and have secured multiple bridging loans and land/development loans in my time.

A broker will talk you through the different funding options, help you decide whether a bridging loan or development financing is most appropriate, and then shop around to find the best deal. Plus, they'll help you complete all the paperwork and present a compelling, professional application that really sells the lender on your project.

PRO TIP

Always work with an independent broker, as opposed to one that's affiliated with a particular lender. And be sure to choose a broker with experience of development financing and bridge loans – not a residential mortgage broker.

How can you find a good broker? Wherever possible, I like to get personal recommendations from people I know and trust, and that's always a good starting point. Failing that, you can search for brokers in your area. Just be sure to do your due diligence, check out their reviews online, and check that they are accredited by the appropriate authority. In the UK, that generally means the Financial Conduct Authority and/or the Association of Mortgage Intermediaries.

Feel free to chat to multiple brokers before you decide which one you want to work with – but, crucially, don't sign up to anything or allow a broker to start making applications or credit checks on your behalf *until* you're sure you want to work with them. If you've got multiple brokers submitting duplicate applications and credit checks, it can affect your credit score.

DIPPING YOUR TOE INTO MORE CREATIVE FINANCING OPTIONS

One of the problems with sticking purely to traditional financing – or indeed, funding developments out of your own pocket – is that you can quickly run out of investment capital, the upfront cash needed to secure favourable loan terms and bag great sites quickly. That's why as a young investor, I soon learned to tap into more creative financing options – or, what I like to call, investing with other people's money.

Strictly speaking, of course, any mortgage or loan is 'other people's money', since you're borrowing the bank's money. But here I'm referring specifically to building relationships with investors who are willing to invest directly in you. Two of the best ways of doing this are through:

- Joint venture (JV) partnerships
- Private lending

Some developers have also had success with crowdfunding their developments, but it's not a route I've explored personally.

PRO TIP

Learning to harness these creative funding options is hands-down one of the most powerful ways to accelerate your property development career. Fairly early in my career, I partnered up with a JV investor to fund a project, and it turned out to be one of those decisions that forever changes your life (in a good way). Not only did this step enable me to expand my ambitions, my JV partner and I ended up collaborating on multiple projects and, ultimately, starting a successful property business together. We still co-own that business to this day. Which demonstrates how important it is to cultivate good relationships with your investors. You never know where it could lead you . . .

If you're going down a joint venture or private lending route, you typically wouldn't work with a broker to secure the deal. You'd seek out and approach potential funders yourself, with the help of a solicitor to draw up the official paperwork. (There are intermediaries who can match those seeking funding with investors, but I prefer to seek out investors myself.) Therefore, this is certainly more advanced than applying for a bridging loan or development financing.

Now, let's delve into JVs and private lending in a little more detail.

Joint venture partnerships

This was my first step into more creative financing options, and it's been a successful financing strategy for me ever since.

A JV is essentially any business enterprise that two (or more) parties enter into, while still retaining their separate entities. This means you don't necessarily have to form an official company together (although you might, purely as the investment vehicle) - rather, your business relationship focuses purely on the deal at hand, such as a specific development project. Your JV partner could be a friend who wants to invest in you, or an external investor that you didn't know before.

PRO TIP

Even if your JV partner is someone you already know, always have a proper JV agreement drawn up by a solicitor to set out the terms of your deal. This should include: what is expected of each party in terms of division of labour, how much (if any) each partner is contributing financially, how the financial rewards will be divided at the end of the project (usually expressed as a percentage), when the parties can expect their money back, and what happens if either party wants to exit the agreement early (including how much notice is required).

With a JV arrangement, the general idea is that both partners are bringing something to the table in terms of expertise, effort and/or money – meaning you both make a positive contribution to the project and you both get a positive outcome.

Beyond that general principle, JVs are completely flexible in terms of how you divvy up the effort, financial input and rewards. For example:

- One partner (your investor) could provide all the cash while the other (you) contribute the expertise and handle the development project.
- You could team up with someone who has a plot of land but doesn't know how to develop it. (In fact, I'm regularly offered deals by landowners who want me to develop their land.) So, your JV partner contributes the land, you bring the development expertise, and you split the development costs and profits.

- Likewise, you could partner with someone who has an existing property that is ripe for development.
- You could even do a JV with a contractor, where you arrange buying the site, planning permission, etc. and they handle every aspect of the build.
- Taking it to an even more advanced level, you could potentially combine two JVs in one project - partnering with a landowner or property owner to develop their site, then partnering with a contractor to get the job done. You then sit somewhere in the middle, acting as go-between and overseeing the project.

When it comes to sharing the profits at the end of the project, there's no one-size-fits-all approach. The profits can be shared equally, or not, depending on how much effort each party has put into the project. You could, for example, agree a 60/40 split in your JV partner's favour, if they're bringing expertise as well as money. Or, if your investor wants to remain entirely hands off and just wants a decent return on their investment, you could potentially go as far as 90/10 in your favour. It's a negotiation at the end of the day, and the goal is to arrive at something that works for both parties.

PRO TIP

Always treat your JV partner's money as if it were your own. Your reputation is on the line here and if you want to do business with this investor or others in future, you need to deliver the agreed outcome. In other words, don't enter into a JV partnership unless you're sure of your ability to successfully deliver the project.

Working with private lenders

Private lending is similar to a JV partnership in the sense that you partner with an individual (or business entity) to fund your project. However, private lending is a *loan agreement* rather than a partnership arrangement. This means the private lender will not usually have any control over the project itself, whereas a JV partner might want to be involved or expect to be consulted on key decisions.

With private lending, the lender is loaning you a defined amount of money, for a defined amount of time, and with a defined amount of interest - just as with any other loan. So, rather than sharing the profits with the lender, as you would with a JV, you're repaying the loan and interest. (The interest being the lender's return on investment). And as with most loans, private lending is secured against the asset in question, meaning if you default on the loan, your lender can take charge of the property.

All of these terms must be set out in a formal loan agreement. This agreement should also stipulate how and when the loan is to be repaid, what happens if you want to repay the loan early, and what happens if you can't make repayments. It's really important to have a formal loan agreement, even if your lender is a friend or family member. And it's important this loan agreement complies with the Financial Conduct Authority's regulatory requirements.

Where to find potential JV partners and private lenders

Finding suitable JV partners and private lenders is the hard part - especially when you're still at the stage of building your reputation as a professional property developer. The truth is, it becomes easier to secure funding through JVs and private lending once you've got more experience securing these types of deals (talk about chicken and egg!). But it's certainly not impossible for those who are still at the 'passionate amateur' end of the scale to score a JV partner or private investor. In fact, that's what I managed to do when I was still fairly early in my career.

A good place to start is with people you already know - either in the development industry (contractors, landowners, property owners) or simply friends and family who might be willing to back you. You can also spread the word among the professionals you work with - for example, your solicitor, architect, estate agent, financial adviser, broker, etc. - that you're actively looking for investors who want a good return on their investment.

Beyond that, you'll need to work hard to continually build your professional network. Which means:

- Attending networking meetings (ideally property-specific networking meetings, if that's an option near you, but generic business networking meetings may also be useful for connecting with potential investors).
- Going to national and regional property exhibitions.
- Using LinkedIn to connect with other property professionals. Be sure to tailor your profile to show your development expertise.
- Joining online property groups and forums.
- Writing helpful contributions on forums, online communities (like wealthlabs.co.uk), LinkedIn and other social media groups to demonstrate your expertise as a property developer. (Investors are often lurking in the background on these sites.)
- You might even consider paying for adverts online and on property forums to attract investors to your cause.
- It's also a good idea to have a professional website that you can point new contacts to. Here, they can learn more about you, get a feel for your previous projects and experience, and connect with you for more info.

You may need to be patient. It takes time to build your network and reputation as a serious developer. But trust that there are investors out there ready to invest in good deals.

Approaching potential JV partners and private lenders with a proposal

Having found a potential investor, you'll need to sell them on the merits of partnering with you or lending to you. This means creating a compelling proposal that sells you as a developer and makes a clear financial case for investing in your project.

This should cover:

- Acquisition costs. This is all the costs involved in purchasing the property/land, including things like stamp duty, legal fees and agent's commission.
- Development costs. Be conservative here, and be sure to build in a contingency.
- Outcome of the project. As in, will the property be sold, or will you retain it and rent it out? What is the expected return on investment (again, be realistic here and don't make promises you can't keep)? And how might the profits be shared? In the case of approaching a private lender, remember their return on investment is interest earned, so you don't need to offer a profit share.

PRO TIP

As your reputation and experience grows, you can create a glossy prospectus to send out to investors, rather than creating a fresh proposal for each project and investor.

A quick word on developer loan notes

Some companies specialise in offering loan notes to investors who are looking to invest in new developments.

A developer loan note is a promissory agreement - basically, an 'I owe you' - between a developer and an investor. In the case of our loan notes, the investor makes a loan to the developer (i.e. my company), and the developer then pays annual returns to the investor (because we retain many of our developments for rental income). Alternatively, a loan note can specify that the developer will repay the loan by a certain date, with a certain amount of interest.

Loan notes allow investors to partner with developers and receive an entirely passive return on their investment (typically 8-12% annual returns). Meanwhile, the developer benefits from another way to raise capital and get developments off the ground. It's important to note that developer loan notes are complex financial products that are tightly regulated by the Financial Conduct Authority, and they should only be marketed to high net worth individuals and sophisticated investors. But it's certainly worth keeping developer loan notes in mind as you look to scale up your development career.

CASE STUDY: SHERWOOD HOUSE, NEWBURY, BERKSHIRE

The project

Conversion of an office building for residential use, creating 27 micro-studios.

The details

We purchased this site and funded the development using a land and development loan. But, with a purchase price of £1.4 million and development cost of £1.5 million, we needed an extra top-up to cover the equity (deposit) portion (an initial instalment due to the builder before receiving the development loan). This top-up came in the form of a loan note from a private lender, organised through my company Redbrick Wealth.

Upon completion, the site was valued at £3.9 million, representing a £1 million profit. But importantly, the strategy here was to create a build-to-rent site for income generation. At the time of writing, the site delivers a total annual gross income of £267,000, which enables us to provide a healthy annual return for our lender.

The key takeaway

Never underestimate how loan notes, private lending or even a JV partnership can help you further your development career and take on larger, higher-value projects.

CHAPTER 5

SOURCING THE BEST DEVELOPMENT OPPORTUNITIES, AND GETTING DEALS DONE

Being able to find great development opportunities, ideally *before* they hit the open market - as opposed to simply trawling property websites for the latest listings - is critical if you want to level up your property development game. Sourcing off-market, as I call it, is a strategy I use all the time to gain an edge over my competitors, so that's my main focus here.

But sourcing great development opportunities is about more than just unearthing properties or plots of land that are ripe for development. You also need to be able to assess potential sites thoroughly. (Note that, for ease, I'll often use the word 'site' to refer to both plots of land and existing buildings - both are covered here.) After all, if you buy the wrong site, or invest in the wrong location, then it doesn't matter how much value you add, you may not achieve the successful outcome you planned.

And, once you've found a great site, done your due diligence and made an offer, there are certain ways you can get a head start on your development project before you formally exchange on the deal. All of this is covered in this chapter, and more.

But let's start with some overarching location considerations.

DECIDING YOUR SEARCH RADIUS

First thing's first, your developments need to be within a reasonable drive of where you live, and this will inform your general search area. Even though you'll have a project manager handling the day-to-day business on site (see Chapters 7 and 8 for more on this), you'll still need to attend site meetings once a month at least. In other words, choosing a site in Newcastle, when you live on the south coast might not be feasible.

PRO TIP

At this stage in my career, I can be relatively hands-off with my developments. But I still typically search for opportunities within one or two hours' drive of where I live. Spending hours driving between sites isn't a good use of my time, and I'd urge you to think carefully about how much time you really want to spend in your car before you settle on a general search area.

Obviously, you might need to be flexible about this if you live in an extremely rural part of the country with not many development opportunities close by.

You'll also need to think about your preferred exit strategy when deciding on your search radius (circle back to Chapter 2 for more on deciding your end strategy). For example, are you developing to sell or are you looking for build-to-rent opportunities? And what is your intended target audience? Do you want to develop flats or micro-studios for young professionals, for instance, or are you targeting the high-end executive home audience?

All of this will inform the general location in which you choose to search for opportunities.

Later on, once you've identified potential deals, you'll need to consider each site's location in more detail – specifically, how it will work for your intended target audience. There's more on assessing a site's location coming up but, for now, I just wanted to stress that there's no point searching in areas that don't work for your end strategy and your work-life balance.

WHAT TYPES OF PROPERTY ARE RIPE FOR DEVELOPMENT?

If the idea of building from scratch floats your boat, I talk more about buying land later on. However, as most small-to-mid-size developers are looking for existing properties to develop, let's start here.

It goes without saying that the type of property you search for will depend on your end strategy and target audience. But remember, whatever type of property you're looking for, you're looking for ways to *add value*.

In my experience, some of the best opportunities to add value are found in:

- Unloved, poorly maintained properties.
- Properties that don't seem to match the local demographic, such as a small office block on an otherwise residential street (which could be converted into flats), or a large house in a busy urban area populated by young professionals (which could make a great HMO opportunity).

- Properties that have stood vacant for a while - including commercial properties that could be converted for residential use (subject to planning, See Chapter 6).
- Older commercial properties - particularly older office buildings and care homes - in an area where new developments are making such older buildings redundant. In many cases, the cost of bringing an older building like this up to the same standard as a new build is prohibitive, which makes them less appealing to commercial buyers and tenants. You can find some great deals this way.

I'm a big fan of converting commercial properties for residential use. Where I live, in the south of England, demand for housing among young professionals is huge, and there simply aren't enough affordable residential properties to go around. (Which is partly why planning laws have been relaxed to allow 'permitted development' on certain types of commercial buildings - read more about this in Chapter 6.)

PRO TIP

Commercial buildings are not as hard to convert for residential use as you might think. In fact, given the scale and internal layout of many commercial buildings, it's often easier to convert them into flats than it is to convert an existing residential building.

Although I largely focus on converting larger offices and care homes (purely because that ties in with the scale of developments I like to take on at this stage in my career), there are smaller offices and care homes out there that are crying out for development. These sorts of projects would be ideal for a developer who's got a few straightforward developments under their belt and is looking to take on higher-value projects.

Of course, offices and care homes aren't the only types of commercial buildings out there. Subject to planning, any type of building could potentially be developed for residential use. For example:

- Pubs provide great opportunities that are really manageable in size. It seems more and more pubs are struggling to survive in the current times.
- Hotels and guest houses, particularly older properties that no longer work as a going hospitality concern.
- Light industrial buildings, such as warehouses and storage facilities. This is an area I'm keeping an eye on. In times of economic hardship, you can see a lot of these types of buildings coming to market.
- Shops. Likewise, this is another potentially very exciting growth area for developers. With the sheer number of empty retail units on Britain's high streets, I reckon this could become a boom category for developers – especially as more planning red tape is eliminated.

SOURCING OFF-MARKET DEALS

Sourcing off-market means you're finding opportunities *before* they're advertised for sale in the usual places. Most of the best deals of my career have come from off-market sources.

Typically, sourcing off-market deals will mean you're approaching property owners and landowners direct or building a name for yourself among local estate agents so that they call you as soon as suitable sites come their way, before they're listed on the open market.

The benefit of finding deals this way is you get ahead of your competitors. If you can move quickly and get an offer accepted before a site ever hits the open market, there's less chance of other developers finding out about it and trying to outbid you.

PRO TIP

Here are some of my favourite ways to source opportunities before they come onto the open market. These can be applied to both sourcing land and sourcing existing properties (commercial or residential).

Approaching property owners and landowners directly

Great development opportunities will always attract other hungry developers, so you want to do whatever you can to get the jump on your competitors. For me, this means going directly to the people who own suitable sites - or encouraging them to come to me.

There are several ways you can do this:

- You can scout your target area and identify specific properties or plots of land that suit your end strategy, then approach the owner directly to see if they might be interested in selling up. You can drop a letter or flyer through the door, for example.
- If lots of local properties fit your bill, you'll need to narrow down your options to those where the owner is more likely to be interested in selling. Vacant buildings fit this bill perfectly.

- You might also like to look at suitable buildings that are advertised for rent. If they've been vacant for a while without earning rental income, the owner may be more open to cashing out.
- You can also encourage property and landowners to approach you directly, by sending out letters or flyers saying that you're a private investor looking for sites to develop (be clear on which types of property or land you're looking for).
- You could also invest in online, social media or local newspaper ads targeting owners in a specific area.
- Also spread the word among your existing network of property professionals - including building contractors, architects, your solicitor, etc. They may know of people in their own network who might be thinking of selling up. You could always offer a finder's fee for introductions that lead to a successful purchase.

Whenever you contact owners or advertise for properties, be sure to stress the benefits of selling directly to you, i.e. a quick sale, at a fair price and with no agent's commission. You'll also need to be able to present yourself as a professional developer, which means you should have business cards, a business-like email address and, ideally, a professional website.

PRO TIP

Make sure you work out the potential market value or income value of a specific property before you approach the owner. This way, you'll have a good idea of what you might be prepared to pay for the property – which, if they're interested, is bound to be one of the first questions they ask! Circle back to Chapter 4 for more on valuation methods.

Sourcing directly like this does require an investment of your time, but it's well worth it. You'll get to know your target area much more deeply, build more of a name for yourself as a local developer, and save on acquisition costs. That said, there is value in working with local agents. Which brings me to . . .

Cultivating strong relationships with local estate agents

This goes beyond simply signing up for an agent's mailing list (although, you should do that as well). You want to get to know agents in your area who specialise in the types of site you're looking for, and regularly check in with them on what's happening in the local market and which sites have come their way.

Why bother doing this? A good estate agent will proactively approach investors and developers before they advertise a property through regular channels (because if they can secure a quick sale without having to go through the faff of marketing a property, it's easy money for them). By building relationships with local agents, they'll keep you in mind and give you a call when a sweet deal comes their way - meaning you can still get ahead of your competitors.

PRO TIP

I've found some great deals by building relationships with commercial estate agents – even though I almost always develop for residential use. This has been a good strategy for me because a lot of commercial agents don't necessarily understand the potential value of a site from a residential perspective.

For this tactic to work, you need to build a reputation for yourself as a serious investor, not a timewaster. So, when a good lead comes your way via an agent, do everything you can to move fast and prove that you are able to commit to and complete deals. Do this, and you'll find more and more opportunities come your way before they hit the open market.

Working with a reputable sourcing agent

I've seen a few deal-sourcing websites, like Dealsourcr, spring up lately and they can be a decent way to find deals. Alternatively, you can connect with specialist sourcing agents on LinkedIn.

PRO TIP

Whenever you work with a sourcing agent to find deals (or even with an estate agent for that matter), always be very specific about the types of sites you're looking for. For example, I might specify that I'm looking for an office building in the Newbury area, of up to 10,000 square feet, with a purchase price of up to £2 million. Giving clear instructions like this helps to mark you out as a serious investor.

ASSESSING DEVELOPMENT OPPORTUNITIES

There are a number of things you'll need to look at when assessing potential development sites, and these broadly fall into:

- The property's (or plot of land's) specific location
- The building itself (or plot of land)
- Cost to develop the site
- Financial viability and gross development value (GDV)

Let's look at each area in turn.

The location

You can't just make your chosen strategy work anywhere. A property or plot of land has to be in the right area for your target market. If you're planning to create flats or studios aimed at young professionals, for example, the property needs to be in an area where there's a ready supply of young professionals who need accommodation. In which case, you'll need to consider the sorts of employers in the area, whether they attract your chosen demographic, and whether there's enough demand for housing among your target audience. (You may not want to develop in a location where the market is already oversupplied with that sort of property.)

Or if you're targeting families, is the location suitable for that audience? Is it relatively quiet (as in, not smack in the city centre)? Are there other families living in the area? What about schools?

PRO TIP

Really do your homework on the local demographics before you commit to a project, especially if you don't know the area that well. (If you tackle multiple projects in the same local area, you will naturally come to understand the local demographics.) As a minimum, research the local population's average age and income, and whether the population is growing. Mouseprice.com is a good starting point for local information.

To assess supply and demand, you can talk to local estate agents (specialising in sales or rentals, depending on your end strategy) to gauge whether properties are being snapped up quickly, and whether a lot of similar properties are coming onto the market.

You'll also want to assess the local area in terms of sale/rent prices. Sites like Rightmove and Zoopla will give you a rough comparison. This is important for assessing the project's financial viability (more on this coming up later).

A few other tips for evaluating a property's or plot of land's location:

- Remember that transport links are important, especially if you're targeting a younger demographic because they may not own cars. Depending on your location, transport links to London may be desirable as well.
- Look at local amenities, such as shops, schools, bars and restaurants (depending on what is likely to be most desirable to your audience).
- Consider who lives in the vicinity and whether they're likely to object to your proposed development. (Neighbours have rarely posed a problem on my developments, but it's worth considering.)
- Look at neighbouring buildings, too, because if the property is located next to a listed building or in a conservation area, it may limit what you can do.
- Also consider local planning restrictions. Particularly if you're planning to change the use of a property under permitted development, you'll need to check that the local authority hasn't removed permitted development rights (which means full planning permission will be required). It's not necessarily a dealbreaker if there are planning restrictions, but you'll need to be aware of this up front. See Chapter 6 for more on planning.

The building itself

Location is critical, so I'd always start with that. But once you're happy that a site's location suits your strategy, then you can assess the building itself. (I'm focusing on assessing an existing building here, but there are tips for assessing a plot of land coming up next.)

At this stage, I would usually look at things like:

- Layout. I start by looking at the building's floorplans to see whether it's conducive to my intended use. I'd say this is probably the most important part of assessing a building, especially if you're changing the use of a property (converting from commercial to residential, for example). My golden rule is: if I can't see how the layout would work within five minutes, it generally means the building isn't right for me.
- Parking. This becomes especially important when you're building multiple units on one site. In my experience, attitudes to parking vary from council to council. Some will expect a site to include a set number of parking spaces according to the number of units in the development. Meanwhile, other councils actively want to discourage the use of cars and would rather you put in bicycle stores. A planning consultant will be able to help you gauge the local council's attitude to parking (see Chapter 6 for more on working with a planning consultant).
- Utilities. When you're working with an older building, especially when you intend to change the use of the building, you may need to upgrade the mains utilities coming into the building. For example, if you plan to convert a commercial building for residential use, the existing building may not have gas mains, which can be really expensive to fit (especially if it involves digging up lots of road). Or the water could be undersupplied (as in, designed to service one toilet per floor instead of multiple flats). In most cases, this stuff isn't a dealbreaker, but it's good to know what you're getting yourself into.
- Façade and roof. Again, if the façade or roof needs work it's probably not a deal breaker, but it can help you negotiate a lower sale price.
- Foundations. You'll obviously have a survey done before buying a property, but you still want to carry out some early due diligence when assessing a property. In particular, be on the lookout for any signs of subsidence, such as cracking in the walls, or evidence of recent redecoration that could be covering something up.

- Asbestos. You're unlikely to encounter major asbestos problems in most buildings, so this is more of a consideration when you're looking at an industrial building (where, potentially, an entire roof could be made of asbestos). Asbestos can be expensive to deal with so, if you're concerned, you could ask the seller to provide an asbestos report.

PRO TIP

It goes without saying that buying a freehold property is preferable to leasehold. But even on a freehold property, you should also find out whether there are any restrictive covenants on the property, which might prevent you from doing certain things without permission. You can usually find out whether there are any restrictive covenants by getting a copy of the title deeds from the Land Registry.

As your experience grows and you become more expert at developing particular types of properties (see Chapter 2), you'll be better able to judge these factors yourself. But when you're new to developing a certain type of property, it's a good idea to get expert help with this.

A good project manager will help you assess potential development sites and, if needed, arrange for specialists to assess the site. (Read more about the importance of partnering with a project manager in Chapter 7.) Failing that, you could have a builder look at the site with you.

And if you have a property development mentor (see Chapter 11), they will also be able to help you assess the suitability of sites.

Assessing land opportunities

If you're looking at plot of land, then there are a whole different set of factors to consider. Here, I would usually start by checking the planning status of the land to see whether it has full planning permission to build on, or outline planning permission (which outlines whether a proposed development would be acceptable to the local authority), or no planning permission at all.

Keep in mind that if the land has outline planning permission, then full planning permission must be sought within three years of outline permission being granted. Obviously, if it has no planning permission at all, then obtaining consent could be a lengthy and costly process. Saying that, it's often easier to get planning permission on a plot of land that has been developed before - say, if it has an old commercial property or derelict building on the site. Getting permission to build a new property on the same footprint can be easier.

I would also investigate the following:

- Are there any restrictive covenants that may impact the intended use of the land?
- Does the council have any investment plans in the surrounding area, which may or may not affect the desirability of the end product?
- Can utilities be provided to the site, and would they have to cross neighbouring land?
- Are there access points?
- Are there any rights of way (such as public footpaths) that cross the land?
- Where exactly do the boundaries lie?
- Are there any other complicated factors such as telegraph poles, manholes, protected trees and flood plains?

A chartered surveyor should be able to help you assess factors like these.

If you're serious about developing land, you should look to establish good connections with your local council's planning office. Always discuss your ideas with them at the outset and work with them to steer your plans. Also work with owners of neighbouring land and properties to get them on board with your plans. If your development will negatively impact neighbours, do everything you can to avoid or mitigate this.

Development costs

One of the key parts of assessing whether a project is right for you is working out how much you think it's going to cost to pull it off. The scale of development costs will also impact how you decide to finance the project (circle back to Chapter 4).

In other words, if you want to reduce your risk of buying a lemon, you need to get a rough ballpark idea of costs before you make an offer. These costs won't be exact (you'll get detailed quotes during the pre-construction phase, see Chapter 7) - and you have to allow for the fact that even ballpark costs will deviate by a certain percentage (say, 10%) - but they do need to be realistic.

At this point in my career, I've done dozens of developments of similar kinds, so am pretty good at doing an initial ballpark costing myself. So I'll start with a basic 'back of the envelope' figure, based on previous projects of a similar nature and average cost per square foot. Then, I'll work with my project manager to build that into a slightly more detailed ballpark figure (looking at factors such as whether we'd need to upgrade the mains utilities on this project, and so on).

If you're not confident at doing even a back of the envelope costing yourself - which you might not be if you haven't tackled that type of building before – it's not a problem. You could get a couple of decent-sized contractors to give ballpark quotes based on cost per square foot.

PRO TIP

Alternatively, you could appoint a quantity surveyor to give you an initial rough costing. Yes, this will cost you money, but if you're serious about becoming a full-time property developer, you have to spend money to make money. To put it bluntly, don't be a tight-arse. Getting a realistic ballpark development cost reduces your risk as a developer, so don't scrimp on this stage.

Once you've made an offer, and you start getting pre-construction consultants on board (see Chapter 7), your costs will become more accurate – and, importantly, they should come down, if you've got a good quantity surveyor on board.

Remember to include the cost of actually acquiring the site, including professional fees and stamp duty (if applicable), in with your development costs.

Financial viability and gross development value (GDV)

As well as costs, you also need to work out how much the site will be worth once the development is completed. This end value will inform how much you're prepared to pay for the site, how much you can actually afford in development costs and even how much you can expect to borrow from a lender. This is why the art of valuation is so important to sourcing good properties. (Circle back to Chapter 4 to learn more about the different ways properties are valued.)

A simple way to calculate whether a site is financially viable is:

Profit = GDV - (Construction + fees + land) + any finance costs

In this formula:

- 'GDV' is gross development value, or the amount you think the site will be worth after development.
- 'Construction' is obviously the cost of developing the site.
- 'Fees' refers to the professional fees and transaction costs.
- 'Land' refers to the purchase price (whether it's land or an existing property).

In other words, you take your estimated end value of the site and then minus everything it costs to buy and develop the site. Only then can you decide whether a site is really worth your time and effort.

PRO TIP

As mentioned in Chapter 2, always look for ways to boost your GDV and make a potential development more valuable. One successful way I've done this is through parking. I know it's not glamorous, but parking is valuable, especially in a busy town centre where parking spaces can be rented out. So when assessing potential sites, consider whether you can add value through monetising parking. Alternatively, if the site has a large area for parking, there may even be scope to develop on some of the parking area.

DOING THE DEAL

Once you're satisfied that the site is financially viable and suits your end strategy, it's time to make an offer.

Negotiating the price

You'll already have a strong idea of the site's value, based on the appropriate valuation method (see Chapter 4) and how you intend to use the site. This will inform your offer.

If you've sourced the site directly and it hasn't yet hit the open market, you may have some leeway to offer less than the site's market value (while still being fair and reasonable - successful property development is about creating win-win scenarios, not screwing people out of money). Equally, if you really want to secure a cracking site and the market is quite competitive, you might be willing to offer higher than market value (when you're certain your end value, after you've developed the site, allows for this).

You'll also want to do whatever you can to sweeten the deal for the seller and encourage them to accept your offer, rather than talk to other developers. For me, this means emphasising my credentials as a developer and my ability to complete on deals.

Getting ahead on certain tasks before you exchange contracts

In my experience, one factor that separates amateur property developers from serious developers is how much they're willing to get done between having an offer accepted and exchanging contracts.

For example, I'll often submit a planning application within days of having an offer accepted (which could be several weeks before I actually exchange on the deal). I do this because planning applications take at least 56 days (for permitted development prior approvals, longer for full planning permission). If I wait until I own the site to do this, then I'm potentially servicing an expensive loan for months while nothing happens on site.

I'll also frequently get started on various surveys and assessments needed at the design stage - such as drainage assessment, fire assessment and acoustic assessment.

PRO TIP

Pressing ahead on certain tasks between offer and exchange will speed up your development schedule enormously. Obviously, there is some element of risk to this – you're paying out for tasks on a site that you don't yet own. But it's a calculated risk. Many of these pre-exchange tasks will actually help to de-risk the development for you because it means you can check out potential problems before you buy the site.

There's no one-size-fit-all approach to this - ultimately, it's up to you how much work you're prepared to do and how much you're prepared to spend before you've exchanged on the deal. The case study at the end of the chapter gives a good example of the types of tasks I'm comfortable doing before I've exchanged on a property.

Yes, this is all upfront spend, but I don't see it as wasted money because all of this pre-exchange work means I'm more comfortable to exchange on the deal, and ready to start the build once the deal is completed. There is a risk that the seller will pull out, or that another developer will come along and gazump me - in which case, I lose the money spent - but it's a risk I'm willing to take.

Of course, if there's no pressure to complete the project quickly, you can do everything post-exchange if you're more comfortable with that.

When deals fall through

Deals don't fall through that often, but it does happen. Every now and then one of my deals might not make it to exchange - but this could be for a number of reasons. My pre-exchange due diligence work might have turned up a huge, expensive problem that means the project is no longer viable. Or planning permission might have been denied (which is why I often like to make an offer 'subject to planning' - more on this in Chapter 6). Obviously you want to minimise the instances of you pulling out of deals, since it can affect your reputation. But when you discover a project is no longer viable, be prepared to abort the deal.

And of course there are times when another developer will come along and swipe the rug out from under your feet. I've been gazumped on a project in the last year. But it's not as common as you might think - especially when you source your own deals off-market, because other developers won't know about the site.

I've also had one deal where the seller simply changed their mind. They decided to get planning permission themselves and list the site with a higher sale price! It's annoying when this happens, but you just have to chalk to up to experience and move on to the next great deal.

Remember, exchange isn't the same as completion. You can get as far as exchanging contracts and still fail to complete the deal, but at least once you've exchanged contracts the vendor can't pull out easily.

PRO TIP

If you're buying a commercial property, one thing that catches a lot of investors out is business rates. Once you've secured a commercial property, it's really important to delist it from business rates as soon as you can. Ordinarily, this will mean you'll have to strip out the building so it can't be used for its former commercial use before you can delist it.

CASE STUDY: SOUTHERN COURT, READING, BERKSHIRE

The project

Commercial to residential conversion, creating 32 micro-studios across two sites (9 and 10 Southern Court).

The details

As soon as my offer was accepted on this site, and before we had exchanged contracts, I got started on several critical tasks:

- This site fell under permitted development, so full planning permission wasn't needed for the conversion. However, I did have to submit a prior approval application (see Chapter 6). The local authority has 56 days to consider any prior approval application and, as you can imagine, this can cause a delay at the start of any project. So within one week of having my offer accepted, I had my architect draw up basic layout floorplans (different to full, detailed design drawings) so that my planning consultant could submit the prior approval application. This meant we'd be ready to get started on the development when the deal was completed.
- Then I had a full building structural survey done, and my project manager arranged for all the relevant surveys needed to complete the pre-construction design work (drainage survey, mechanical and electrical survey, etc. - read more about pre-construction in Chapter 7). I also had a quantity surveyor work up a more detailed ballpark development cost based on the results of the surveys.
- Next, I got the architect to draw up the in-depth design drawings. Different to the planning floorplans, these detailed drawings are needed for building control approval, and for getting accurate

quotes from contractors. Because these drawings can take several weeks, this was another key area where I wanted to get ahead.

- The project manager and I could then invite contractors to tender for the project so we could get accurate, full costings.
- And, of course, I worked with my broker on the finance application, and booked the evaluation survey for development financing purposes.

This is a pretty typical example of what I might do *before* the seller and I have even exchanged contracts. On some projects, I may even do more than this – for example, if full planning permission is required, that takes more work.

The key takeaway

Spending money on these tasks pre-exchange was a calculated risk I was willing to take because it meant we could get going on the build as soon as we completed the deal.

CHAPTER 6

TACKLING THE PLANNING PROCESS

It may seem odd to have a chapter on planning before we've even talked about the design and other pre-construction elements of your project (see Chapter 7). However, since planning is arguably one of the highest-risk elements of developing, and a meaty subject in its own right, I'm covering it here rather than lumping it in with the rest of pre-construction.

Planning is one of those areas where the rules change frequently (the National Planning Policy Framework, which sets out the governments planning policies for England, is regularly updated). What's more, different local authorities have different attitudes to development. So consider this an overview of the key planning considerations and strategies to keep in mind as you progress to more complex projects. You'll need expert help to determine which considerations apply to your projects.

BUYING A SITE WITH PLANNING CONSENT VERSUS BUYING WITHOUT

The process of making an offer and buying a site, specifically in relation to planning, will follow one of three routes:

- Buying a site that already has planning consent to develop
- Making a conditional offer, subject to planning
- Buying unconditionally

Let's look at each one in turn.

Buying a site that already has planning consent to develop

This means you don't have to apply for planning permission, since the seller has already sought consent.

The pros:

- You have less hassle up front because you don't have to navigate the planning process.
- Your risk as an investor is lower.

The cons:

- You'll probably pay a premium for the site because the seller has added value by getting the planning permission in place. (They've assumed this risk, and naturally want to be fairly compensated for that.)

PRO TIP

When buying a site that already has permission, it's vital you check that whatever the seller has got consent for is actually legal to build. Planners aren't necessarily thinking about building regulations when they approve a planning application, and building control (building regs) approval is entirely separate from planning permission. If the approved design won't pass building control, then you'll have to revise it and resubmit to planning – which defeats the point of buying a site with permission. Your project manager will help with checking the design meets building regs, often by bringing on board specialist consultants and/or liaising with an approved building control inspector. Read more about building control in Chapters 7 and 8.

Of course, if the planning that's in place isn't workable – or simply doesn't offer enough GDV for your liking (see Chapter 2) – you could always revise the design to your own liking and reapply for planning, obviously adjusting your offer accordingly to take account of the fact that the existing planning isn't suitable.

Making a conditional offer, subject to planning

Here, the site doesn't have planning consent, so you make an offer, but reserve the right to pull out of the deal if you don't get the right planning consent. You then apply for planning before exchanging on the deal (circle back to Chapter 5 for more on this).

The pros:

- A conditional offer lowers your risk in the sense that, if you don't get the permission you want, you can walk away.
- Sites without planning permission are usually a good deal cheaper than sites with permission.

The cons:

- You're taking on the risk of getting planning, which means you're coughing up for the planning drawings, planning consultant (and any other consultants needed at this stage), plus the application itself. If the deal falls through, you don't get this money back.

I prefer to think of this approach as a calculated risk. Yes, there is upfront expense with no guarantee that the property will be yours. However, in my experience, this risk usually pays off.

Buying unconditionally

Again, the site doesn't have planning, but instead of offering subject to planning, you swoop in and make an unconditional offer that's not dependent on a specific planning outcome.

The pros:

- Because you're prepared to absorb the risk that you won't be granted permission, you can get some incredible deals this way. Some of my most successful developments (in terms of profit) have been those where I've offered unconditionally.

The cons:

- You're at the mercy of the local authority on what will be allowed, and also how long it takes to get approval. If you're sat on an expensive bridge loan (see Chapter 4), this is a big consideration.
- And, of course, there's always the risk that your application will be denied, leaving you with a site that you can't develop in the way you intended.

This option isn't for the fainthearted. You need to be pretty damn sure that you will get the permission you want. Every developer has a different risk tolerance, so whether this is an option for you comes down to your individual risk profile. Personally, where I've done similar developments in the same area and am 99% certain I'll get permission, buying unconditionally is a risk I'm happy to take.

WHAT TYPES OF DEVELOPMENT REQUIRE FULL PLANNING CONSENT?

The short answer is, many of them! Certainly when you're building a new build on a plot of land you can expect to apply for full planning consent. And even when you're working with an existing building, full planning consent is often required. As a general rule, any type of conversion or development of an existing building that *doesn't* fall under permitted development (more on this coming up next) will require planning permission.

Getting to grips with planning and permitted development requires a basic understanding of building use classes. Properties in England, whether commercial or residential, are categorised according to use classes. These use classes include:

- Commercial, business and service buildings, such as shops, offices, light industrial buildings, banks, restaurants and cafes – at the time of writing, these fall under use class E.
- Hotels – use class C1.
- Residential institutions (including residential care homes) – use class C2.
- Houses and flats (residential dwellings) – use class C3.
- HMOs of between three and six residents – use class C4.
- Sui Generis use class – which means 'in a class of their own' and refers to buildings that do not fall under other use classes, including public houses, cinemas, theatres and HMOs with more than six residents.

Usually (but not always), you will need planning permission to change a property from one use class to another – for example, if you want to convert a pub into a residential property. The exception to this rule is when something falls under permitted development rights.

PERMITTED DEVELOPMENT

I'm really pleased to see that the current government (at the time of writing) is allowing more types of development under permitted development and generally looking to ease planning red tape. This is essential for encouraging developers to build much-needed housing.

What is permitted development?

Permitted development (PD) refers to rules that are designed to simplify the planning process. Under PD, certain types of property, including some commercial properties, can be converted to certain other use classes without seeking full planning permission. This obviously makes the development process easier and lowers risk for developers.

PD is like Mecca for developers! Even really experienced developers love PD projects because it massively helps to lower the risks involved with developing a property (particularly when you're changing a property's use – for example, converting a commercial building to residential). I do a lot of office-to-residential conversions, largely because they are typically easy to push through under PD rights.

Changes of use that fall under permitted development

PD is *not* allowed on listed buildings, in conservation areas and in areas of outstanding natural beauty. If your site falls under these, regardless of its use class, you'll need to seek full planning permission.

Those exceptions aside, there are a number of changes of use that currently fall under PD. Here are just a few examples (correct at the time of writing) of what's allowed under PD:

- Converting a shop into a residential dwelling (although there is currently a size restriction of up to 150m², and these developments are subject to prior approval – more on prior approval coming up later).
- Converting an office into a residential dwelling (with no size restriction, but subject to prior approval).
- Converting a light industrial building into a residential dwelling (again, with a size restriction up to 150m² and subject to prior approval).
- Converting a dwelling into an HMO of between three and six residents.

PRO TIP

Converting offices into flats, studios and micro-studios makes up a significant portion of my portfolio at present. Because it falls under PD, it's a strategy I'd strongly encourage any developer to explore if they want to take their development career to the next level. What's more, I get a lot of personal satisfaction from turning an older, potentially unused office building into modern, much-needed housing, and I find it to be a more sustainable way of developing, compared to focusing purely on new builds.

I expect to see the next planning shakeup in England further relax PD rights, and remove size restrictions on certain use classes - which would, for example, allow shops of any size to be converted for residential use. Watch this space, and always visit the Planning Portal for the most up-to-date info. Another useful resource is Planning Geek (planninggeek.co.uk), which is great for understanding planning changes.

PRO TIP

Even if your project falls under PD and you don't need to apply for full planning permission, it's likely you'll still have to go through a less stringent approvals process known as 'prior approval'. For this reason, I would still recommend working with a planning consultant.

Going through the prior approval process

Many changes of use under PD are subject to prior approval, which is essentially a drastically cut-down version of full planning permission, focusing on specific factors only. Prior approval allows the local planning authority to assess the likely impacts and risks of your proposed development in terms of factors such as:

- Transport and highways (including impact on local roads and intended parking allocation for the development).
- Flooding risks and impacts of the development.
- Noise impacts on intended occupants (for example, when you're converting an office block into flats you may require acoustic flooring to minimise noise).
- Contamination risks on the site (for example, the risk of contamination from existing oil tanks to intended occupants).
- Other factors such as air quality and the provision of adequate light.

PRO TIP

You may or may not need assessment reports on all of the impact areas listed above, which means employing specialist consultants to carry out assessments for you (for example, one consultant to do a flooding assessment, another to do an acoustic assessment, etc.). The reports and level of detail required will depend on your use class. Your planning consultant will be able to advise on which reports you do and don't need, and your project manager will be able to help you appoint the various consultants.

There are additional restrictions that can be placed on PD projects, depending on the building's current use class, its proposed use class, and its location. These could include the design/external appearance of the building, and sustainability factors.

In other words, even when your proposed development falls under PD, the local authority can, in theory, refuse your application on these grounds (this is a particular risk where the local council is averse to developments in their area), or place restrictions on your development.

Here's how the prior approval process generally works:

- You – or, more likely, your planning consultant – submit basic design drawings (typically floorplans and elevations), plus assessment reports on the required impact areas.
- You can apply for prior approval online through the Planning Portal but, as I've said, I would always employ a planning consultant to help prepare and submit the application.
- The local authority has 56 days to respond from the date of receiving the application (although this can be extended in certain circumstances). It's not uncommon for them to have questions as they consider your request, and your planning consultant will be able to help address these.
- You cannot start work on the project until the prior approval process is complete.

PRO TIP

In theory, prior approval isn't supposed to have conditions attached. But, in practice, councils often do attach conditions, and you'll have to either conform to these conditions or be prepared to argue your point. There's more on planning conditions coming up later in the chapter.

Removal of PD rights

PD rights are country-wide, however, local authorities do have the power to remove PD rights in certain areas using a mechanism called Article 4. If your local authority has invoked Article 4, it means PD rights have been removed, and you'll have to seek full planning permission.

WHEN FULL PLANNING PERMISSION IS REQUIRED

Just because a project requires full planning permission doesn't mean it's off the table, but you'll have to be prepared for the extra risk and hassle involved in seeking planning consent.

Is it worth it?

There are obvious downsides to having to seek planning permission, including:

- It takes time. Securing planning permission can take a lot of time – up to 13 weeks on larger developments, and potentially 16 weeks if an environmental impact assessment is needed. This additional time increases your overall risk on the project, especially if you're servicing an expensive bridge loan.
- It costs money. It should be clear by now that you'll need professional help to navigate the planning process, including hiring an architect to draw up plans, hiring consultants to conduct any necessary assessments, and of course, hiring a planning consultant. All this costs money, but is worth it to ensure a smooth planning process.
- Ultimately, there's no guarantee that your proposed development will be approved. What is your plan B if you're not allowed to use the building in the way you intended? Are you prepared to go down a (potentially) lengthy appeals process? This is why, when offering on a site, I often stipulate that my offer is subject to planning consent. That way I can walk away from the deal if I need to.

The need to apply for full planning permission may or may not be a dealbreaker for you, and that's fine – certainly while you're getting used to taking on bigger projects. It all comes down to your individual risk profile and how confident you are of your dream team (see Chapter 3).

Personally, I don't shy away from projects that require planning permission. In fact, there can be significant advantages to scoring planning permission, because it usually means you're adding significant value to a site.

PRO TIP

Some property investors use securing planning permission as a strategy in its own right. They buy a site cheap without planning, then secure planning permission to convert the existing building or build something new on that site – and this alone can make the site far more valuable. They then sell the site and pocket the profit without having to lay a single brick.

Seeking pre-application advice

This is a great tip if you want to further reduce your risk on a planning application.

Many people aren't aware that you can seek 'pre-application advice' from the local authority if you want to discuss a potential development. This paid-for service allows you to basically sound out the council, meet with a local planning officer to discuss your plans and take the council's temperature to gauge how they feel about your proposal.

PRO TIP

Seeking pre-application advice helps you get a steer on what the council will and won't allow before you go ahead and submit your application – and is particularly worthwhile on contentious or unusual developments. I've taken advantage of this when considering buying potentially contentious sites, and the planning officer's steer has occasionally led to me not buying the site in question, saving me a lot of hassle.

An overview of the planning application process

The typical planning application process unfolds as follows:

- You or your planning consultant apply online via the Planning Portal (or you may be able to submit a paper application to your local authority).
- With the application, you'll have to supply various plans and supporting documents, such as:

  - Existing and proposed floorplans for the interior
  - Existing and proposed exterior elevations, showing the features and design of the property's exterior
  - Any additional reports and assessment that are specific to your site
  - Potentially, mechanical and electrical drawings (M&E) for the installation of main services, like electrics and plumbing

- The local authority will check your application is complete and ask for any missing information. This is known as 'validating' your application, and you'll be notified in writing when your application has been validated.
- Then the local authority will publicise and consult on the application with relevant stakeholders (such as neighbours).
- Next, a planning officer or planning committee will decide on your application. Most applications for smaller developments are decided within eight weeks, but for more complex applications this may be extended to 13 weeks (16 weeks if an environmental impact assessment is needed).
- When a decision has been made, you'll be notified in writing whether consent has been granted (with or without conditions – more about conditions later in the chapter) or refused. If consent is refused, or if you find the conditions of consent unacceptable, you have the right to appeal (more on this coming up).

- Generally, you'll have three years from the date permission was granted to begin your development. After this, planning permission expires.

Finally, remember that planners aren't necessarily considering your proposed design from a building regulations perspective, so it's up to you to ensure that the design you're putting through planning complies with building regs and can legally be built. This may mean you need to appoint various consultants at design stage (for example, a fire strategy consultant) before you submit your planning application.

Believe me, it's much better to do this work up front than to secure planning consent then later find out you need to change your design (which means you need to go back to planning for approval). This is a trap that many developers fall into.

WHY YOU MIGHT WANT TO CONSIDER A TWO-PHASE PLANNING STRATEGY

Where planning isn't straightforward, or you don't think you'll get the outcome you want, it is often possible - with the help of a planning consultant - to achieve your ultimate end goal via multiple planning stages. This forward-thinking tactic is one that I've used myself to achieve an otherwise difficult planning outcome.

In very basic terms, this means you apply for planning permission to change from one use class to another (this is phase one of your planning strategy); then, once you've completed the project and the building is occupied under its new use class, you can, after a bit of time has passed, either apply to change the use class again, or perhaps even take advantage of PD rights (phase two of the planning strategy).

For example, in phase one I might convert a commercial building into residential flats. Having done that, PD rights would mean I could later convert those residential flats into HMO flats - which is better from a rental income perspective because each flat can be rented out to more occupants.

Now, if I try to go straight from commercial building to HMOs in one planning application hit, I would probably come up against resistance from planners, but doing it in two stages means I can achieve my ultimate end goal more easily. Check out the case study at the end of this chapter for a specific example of a two-phase planning strategy.

PRO TIP

Don't disclose your ultimate end goal to the council during your initial planning application. Also, be aware that this tactic isn't without its risks – local authorities can remove PD rights at any time under Article 4, so you need to be confident that your first planning phase works financially as a development, in the event that that's all you can do.

How long do you have to wait between phase one and phase two of your planning strategy? To be honest, it's a bit of a grey area and it varies from council to council. In my experience, it could be as little as six months, but your planning consultant will be able to guide you on this.

DEALING WITH PLANNING CONDITIONS AND PLANNING OBLIGATIONS

In order to approve your application, the local authority may feel the need to attach certain planning conditions or obligations that you need to comply with.

Planning conditions

A planning condition is any condition imposed on a planning approval. This means, rather than refuse an application outright, the local authority grants permission, providing certain conditions are met. The condition could be anything from use of the site (restricted operating hours, for example) to the colour of materials you use on the building's exterior.

These conditions fall into two camps:

- Pre-commencement condition, which means you cannot start work on the project until this condition is resolved (discharged, in planning speak).
- Pre-occupation condition, which means you can crack on with the build but the condition needs to be discharged before people can occupy the building.

PRO TIP

Be aware that planning conditions can apply on PD projects as well as full planning applications. Before submitting your application (whether it's for full planning permission or PD prior approval), your planning consultant should have a fairly good idea of which sort of conditions the council is likely to impose (if any). Failing that, you can always approach the local planning authority to get a steer on potential conditions.

According to the National Planning Policy Framework, planning conditions should only be imposed when they are *necessary* and *relevant*. There's an argument that planning conditions aren't *necessary* or *relevant* on PD projects - the whole point of PD is to remove planning red tape - but local authorities do like to throw their weight around, so it's not uncommon for them to place conditions on prior approvals. In fact, I find this occurring more and more frequently.

If you're unhappy with a planning condition, you can go back to the local authority and argue your case. This, rather than a formal appeal, is often enough to reach a resolution.

For example, on a recent project where I was mentoring a client through their development, the planners attached a pre-commencement condition that said we needed a contamination report on some oil tanks that were located on site *prior* to starting work. But removing the oil tanks and testing for contamination meant we had to physically start work on the site. It was a bit of a catch 22. So we went back to the planners and made our case, and they agreed to amend it to a pre-occupation commencement. This far more reasonable approach meant that we had to check that there was no contamination from the old oil tanks before anyone could occupy the building (and if there was contamination, we had to deal with it before people moved in).

Planning obligations

Permission may also be subject to planning obligations, which are legal obligations designed to mitigate or compensate for any negative impacts of a proposed development. Planning obligations are also commonly called 'section 106 agreements', 'developer contributions' or 'affordable housing contributions'. Of course Permitted Development doesn't have these contributions which makes it all the more attractive!

When a planning obligation is attached to planning permission, it basically means the developer has to contribute something to enhance the local area in return for being granted planning permission. When this applies and exactly what you have to contribute varies from council to council, and according to the size of your development. Your 'contribution' could take the form of a cash payment to help fund local services or, on larger developments, it may even mean you have to give the council a proportion of the units in the development to be used for affordable housing. Obviously, this is more of a consideration when you're building (or converting into) multiple units on one site.

PRO TIP

Another consideration that falls under the developer contributions bracket is the Community Infrastructure Levy (CIL). This is a charge levied by some local authorities on developments, which helps the council pay for infrastructure services to support the development – roads, new bus stops, etc. Depending on your local authority's attitude to developments, any new developments that create an additional 'gross internal area' of 100m^2 or more, or create new dwellings, are potentially liable for CIL. Crucially, this may apply even on PD sites.

If you're unhappy with a planning obligation, and don't get anywhere with the local authority, you can appeal a planning obligation via the Planning Inspectorate (acp.planninginspectorate.gov.uk).

WHEN PLANNING IS DENIED OR DELAYED – THE APPEALS PROCESS

I've mentioned that you can appeal planning conditions and planning obligations that have been attached to planning permission. But what happens if you are denied planning permission altogether? Or if your application isn't determined within the relevant time period?

In these cases, your first port of call is to talk to the local authority about why the application was rejected (or why it is being held up), and whether there's anything you can do to reach a resolution. It may be that you can gain consent by changing your design and resubmitting your application via the Planning Portal, or by agreeing to certain conditions.

PRO TIP

If you aren't already, I strongly advise working with a planning consultant when consent is denied or delayed. They'll be able to approach the local authority on your behalf, and if you need to go down the formal appeals route, they'll guide you through that process.

If you have no joy with the local authority, as a last resort you can make a formal appeal to the Planning Inspectorate. However, according to the Planning Portal, only around one in three appeals are actually successful, so it's important you go into this process with your eyes wide open. Sometimes, you need to know when to cut your losses and move on.

If you want to go ahead with an appeal, the decision notice from your local authority will confirm your rights of appeal and set out how long you have to submit an appeal - usually within six months of the date of the decision, after which you lose your right of appeal.

There are three different types of appeal procedures. When you submit your appeal, you'll be asked which procedure you want to go down, so be sure to work with your planning consultant to determine the most appropriate procedure for your case.

The three procedures are:

- Written representation
- Hearing
- Local inquiry

Let's delve into each one in a little more detail.

Written representation

Most types of appeal are dealt with via this route. Here, the appellant (that's you), the local authority and any other stakeholders submit written evidence, usually in the form of statements. The planning inspector will then consider all the evidence and visit the site, usually with the main parties. (Note that verbal submissions aren't allowed in this route, even when visiting the site with the inspector.) It may be several weeks after the site visit before you get a final decision.

Hearing

This route is similar to written representations, in that the main parties submit written evidence. However, there is then an informal hearing to discuss the case. This usually takes the form of a roundtable discussion between you, the local authority representative, the planning inspector, and any other relevant third parties (such as local residents). The planning inspector leads the discussion, which typically concludes with a site visit. And again, it may be several weeks after the site visit before you get a final decision.

Local inquiry

This is a much more formal procedure, and is usually only appropriate in complex cases where there are legal issues to consider. With this route, the main parties have proper legal representation to make their case and cross-examine witnesses, plus written evidence has to be submitted in advance. Inquiries can take several days or even weeks to complete, and will include a site visit at some point. Again, the decision can take several weeks after the conclusion of the inquiry.

CASE STUDY: HOLMWOOD GARDENS, WALLINGTON, SOUTH LONDON

The project

Conversion of a care home to residential flats and then onto HMO flats, via a two-stage planning process.

The details

We purchased this site as a care home (use class C2, residential institution), with the eventual plan to convert it into HMO flats (use class C4). However, we knew that the local authority wouldn't be open to a straight change of use from C2 to C4 - based on precedent, the application would most likely have been rejected on the grounds of overpopulation. So we decided to adopt a two-stage planning strategy.

In phase one, we converted the C2 property into five regular flats (use class C3, residential dwellings), which was comfortably approved by the local authority. We then later took advantage of PD rights to convert those flats from use class C3 into C4 HMO flats. We had to wait around 6 months to ensure the original planning approval was implemented for a decent amount of time before using these onward PD rights. This was important to avoid the council challenging the approach by saying we'd jumped straight to the end use.

The beauty of this strategy is, under PD, it is possible to change the use of a building from C3 to C4 without having to apply for planning permission, meaning we could more easily create 30 lettable bedrooms on one site - which was our original end goal.

Converting the property for C4 use added significant value and the site was subsequently sold to an HMO operator for a gross profit of £1.3 million.

The key takeaway

We planned this two-phase strategy from the start, and were prepared to play the long game to ultimately get the development we wanted. So when moving immediately from one use class to another isn't possible, consider whether a two-phase planning strategy might get you where you want to be.

And, needless to say, a planning consultant was absolutely invaluable in planning and executing this two-stage strategy.

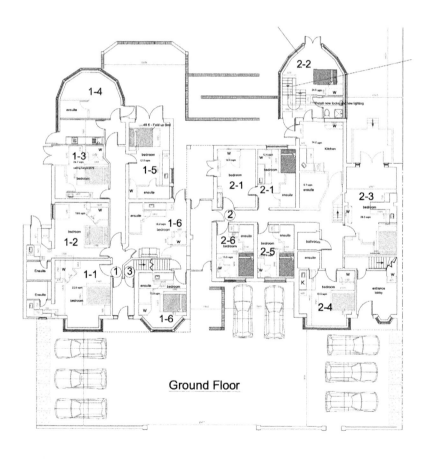

Ground Floor

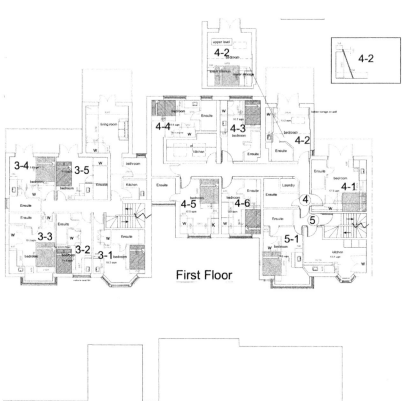

First Floor

Second Floor

CHAPTER 7

GETTING YOUR PROJECT OFF THE GROUND: THE PRE-CONSTRUCTION PHASE

Having sourced a suitable property and got your financing ducks in a row, you're now ready to get the development project underway. While novice developers might immediately turn their thoughts to the construction phase, more experienced developers will know there's much work to be done before a single tradesperson sets foot on site. It's best, then, to think of any development project in terms of three very distinct stages: pre-construction, the construction itself, and finally, post-construction. What happens at the pre-construction stage is just as (if not more) important to the success of your project as the construction itself. Which is why pre-construction deserves a chapter of its own.

Before we get into the specifics, let me stress that each development project is different in terms of size, complexity and requirements. To cover as much as possible, I've written this chapter and the next (which deals with construction and post-construction) with mid-sized to larger developments in mind – such as converting an office building into residential properties, building on a plot of land, or taking on a *substantial* residential conversion or renovation.

Therefore, some of the sections in this chapter may not apply to all of your development projects, and that's fine. It's not a prescriptive framework that you have to follow step by step – rather, it's an overview of key pre-construction considerations. In other words, always be guided by your personal dream team of experts (see Chapter 3) on the best course of action for each specific development.

With that caveat done, let's get into it.

WHAT DO WE MEAN BY PRE-CONSTRUCTION?

Before construction gets underway, you need to present your contractor with viable plans that can go ahead. Lots of prep work is needed to create these viable plans, hence the pre-construction phase.

Of course, on a small, straightforward project – say, refurbishing a house – many of the pre-construction tasks listed below may not apply. You may not even be going out to main contractors for quotes. You might just approach plumbers, electricians and decorators for prices, without the need for detailed drawings. That's on a small project. The bigger the project, however, the more complex the pre-construction phase gets.

On one of my average projects, the pre-construction phase might entail:

• Preparing for legally required health and safety duties under the Construction (Design and Management) Regulations (also known as CDM Regulations). This includes working with designers and consultants to establish health and safety risks, and how these should be addressed, and generally ensuring all CDM requirements are in place.

- Arranging to have relevant surveys and assessment reports carried out.
- Liaising with the designers on the creation of detailed design drawings and monitoring the design process.
- Liaising with neighbours, or serving a legally required Party Wall Notice where appropriate. The courts take a dim view if construction work is started without a Party Wall Agreement being in place.
- Confirming which approvals are needed for the project to go ahead, including arranging and reviewing planning consent (which may or may not stipulate certain conditions on the project, see Chapter 6).
- Gathering all the information needed to form the suite of tender documents (pre-construction information) to be issued to pre-qualified contractors (i.e. contractors that have been deemed capable to carry out the work).
- Inviting tenders for the work and assessing quotes on a like-for-like basis.
- Arranging contracts with the chosen contractor(s).
- Ensuring all relevant warranties and guarantees are in place.
- Checking that contractors have the necessary insurance.
- Appointing an approved building inspector for building control purposes (see Chapter 3).

Sounds like a lot, doesn't it? Many of the pre-construction tasks are about pulling together the relevant design drawings, reports and information needed for the project to go ahead. Depending on the scale of the project, this may include things like architect's drawings, mechanical and electrical (M&E) drawings, fire design specification, acoustic report, contamination report, health and safety risk assessments, approved inspector's plan check and more.

The purpose of all this information is to set out exactly what you intend to build. Obviously, this is crucial from a planning and building regulation (building control) point of view, but it's also crucial from a procurement/tendering perspective. Only once you've pulled together all this information can you invite firms to tender for the work, choose a contractor, and sort out the relevant contract(s) – all of which also fall into the pre-construction phase.

PRO TIP

You can't compare builders' quotes with any confidence if the various contractors are each making different assumptions based on sketchy information. Being absolutely clear on what you want to achieve in your development is the best way to ensure you're getting like-for-like quotes, and, ultimately, the best deal.

Here's a quick example of why this pre-construction stage is so important. My company converted an office building in Newbury into 42 studio apartments. It was a £6.3m GDV (Gross Development Value) project with a £1.95m construction budget. On builds like this, even a small detail can have a big knock-on effect in terms of quotes. At this sort of scale, if you underestimate the number of plug sockets needed (as a very simple example), your electrical quote could be inaccurate by thousands of pounds.

You can see why pre-construction matters to the overall success of your project – and isn't just about getting the right approvals in place. The good news is, a project manager will be able to help you with most of these pre-construction stages (with the exception of planning, for which you'll need a planning consultant).

One seemingly easy way around all of this complexity is to hire a contractor on a 'design and build' basis. In other words, you say to a contractor, 'I want to build X, Y and Z, now go away and design that for me, sort out all the relevant approvals, then build it, please and thank you.' That's one way to do it, and I see why it's an attractive option for novice developers. But, for reasons I'll go into later in the chapter, the design and build route isn't necessarily one I'd recommend.

SHOULD YOU BE YOUR OWN PROJECT MANAGER?

I project managed some of my early development projects, largely because they were pretty small and I wanted to be more hands-on so that I could learn about property development from the inside. To this day, I occasionally still manage the odd small project myself.

For example, if I'm developing a three bedroom house into a five bedroom HMO. This may just be a case of turning a couple of reception rooms into additional bedrooms, upgrading the kitchen and fitting a couple of new bathrooms. On projects like this, where the total spend is less than, say, £30-40k, there's little need for a project manager. It doesn't take a lot of time and effort for me to oversee the work myself. I probably wouldn't even appoint a main contractor in cases like this - I'd just appoint separate tradespeople. However, If you live abroad or have a full time job and want to take on smaller refurbishment projects, a part time project manager may be helpful.

But as I've said, this book assumes you're doing more than just fitting a new kitchen and bathroom suites. In which case, I wouldn't recommend attempting to project manage bigger developments yourself. Not unless you want to become a full-time project manager (which is what will happen on more complex sites).

PRO TIP

This book assumes that you want to become a full-time property developer, not a full-time project manager. And that means handing over the day-to-day oversight of your developments to a professional project manager. After getting my first few (smaller) developments under my belt, I quickly learnt that it was much more profitable to spend my time building my property development business (looking for new opportunities, developing relationships with investors, and so on), than managing the nitty gritty work on site.

That's why I strongly advocate partnering with a project manager, and have written the rest of this chapter (and the next) with that in mind.

Yes, there is a cost associated with hiring a project manager, and you'll need to factor this into your overall budget. But I prefer to think in terms of *value*, not cost. The value I get from employing a project manager is huge in terms of de-risking my projects, making sure projects come in on time and on budget and, ultimately, freeing up my time to focus on finding the next great development opportunity.

There's also a legal argument to appointing an independent project manager. In certain contracts, there's an obligation on the person administering the contract and monitoring progress on the project to act in a reasonable way that's fair to both parties. If that duty falls to you (if you're managing a project yourself), and you end up in a dispute with your builder, it would be very hard to prove that you always acted in a reasonable and fair manner. Yet another reason to appoint an independent third party, in my view.

Professional project managers will also be suitably qualified and experienced, and therefore be able to offer you the appropriate insurance protection. This means you can potentially make a claim should their negligence be shown to be the cause of any losses you may subsequently incur.

WHAT KIND OF PROJECT MANAGER DO YOU NEED?

Historically, the project manager role might have been carried out by the architect. However, over the years, it's become a separate discipline in its own right. And with good reason - expertise on the drawing board doesn't necessarily translate to the construction site. What's more, it's disproportionately expensive to have an architect manage the project (not least because of the cost to the architect of maintaining professional indemnity insurance on something that isn't necessarily considered a core competency for architects).

Which is why you're more likely to work with an independent project manager or project management firm on your developments. But it's important to note that there are different services that come under the scope of project management.

It's perhaps easier to think of project management as an umbrella term covering various different tasks across the pre-construction, construction and post-construction phases. In other words, when you approach project managers or project management firms, you may be presented with a choice of different services:

- Project manager
- Contract administrator
- Employer's agent

There's a fair bit of overlap between these services, and knowing which service you need can be confusing. The best option for you will depend on the building route you're taking - specifically, whether you're appointing a contractor on a 'design and build' basis, or separating out the design and build contracts.

The project management firm that I work with summarises the difference between the roles as follows:

- All pre-contract tasks fall to a *project manager*.
- Then, once you're at the stage of appointing a contractor, the contract administrator *or* employer's agent role kicks in.
- A *contract administrator* will liaise with the contractor and oversee progress on the project. It is possible to retain the services of a project manager for the duration of the project. It's just that the role of project manager usually changes once the contract is placed and construction is underway. Essentially, this distinction in the roles is usually determined by the type, scale and complexity of

the project. For instance, with a Minor Works contract (I talk about the different types of contracts later in the chapter), for a relatively low-value, low-risk development, you're unlikely to need the full range of services, especially with regard to the contract management side of things.

- Or if you're opting for a 'design and build' approach (again, more on this coming up), you will instead need an *employer's agent* to liaise with the contractor on your behalf and oversee progress. I'll explain why soon.

PRO TIP

To clarify, the project manager and contract administrator roles could absolutely be covered by the same person. Likewise, the project manager and employer's agent may be the same person. A good way to think of it is that the project manager's tasks typically cover the very start of the project, whereas the contract administrator or employer's agent tasks kick in only at the stage of appointing the contractor. A professional project management firm will be able to handle all these tasks for you, across the entire lifecycle of the project.

Let's delve into the various tasks in a little more detail.

Project manager

Being involved from the very start of the project, the project manager's key tasks include:

- Agreeing the overall brief and budget with the client.
- Reviewing and mitigating project risks.
- Seeking proposals from designers, surveyors and consultants.

(Or, in the case of a 'design and build' contract, the project manager will invite design and build firms to tender for the project.)

- Reviewing designs and making recommendations to the client.
- Making sure that necessary approvals are obtained and later complied with.
- Researching different contractors and other specialists.
- Agreeing the programme of works (schedule).
- As mentioned, once construction is underway, the project manager might also be monitoring progress and holding regular progress meetings, if the contract is of relatively low risk and value.
- The project manager may also be involved with processing payment requests and passing these to the client once approved.

Contract administrator

Kicking in at the stage of appointing the contractor, this role is about ensuring that both the employer's (client's) and contractor's duties and obligations are discharged in line with the contract. One really important thing to note is that, although a contract administrator is employed by the client, they have an obligation to be fair and make decisions that are best for both parties. Therefore, they may push back on certain client demands or requests that are considered unreasonable.

(Again, you can see why it's difficult to carry out this role yourself, and why it's important to work with a professional. In the case of a dispute, proving that you were always working in a fair and neutral manner for the benefit of both parties, when you yourself are the client, would be practically impossible!)

Key contract administrator tasks include:

- Making sure the contractor has the right insurance before a contract is awarded.
- Administering the contract and issuing instructions.

- Once construction is underway, monitoring progress on site and holding regular progress meetings.
- Arranging handover and obtaining handover documents and warranties.
- Organising snag list and final sign off.

Employer's agent

You'll notice from the following list that many of the employer's agent duties align with some of the contract administrator tasks. However, while a contract administrator is required to act in a fair, neutral manner to both parties, an employer's agent has zero obligations to the contractor and is free to advocate 100% for their client, who they are appointed to represent. This is why the employer's agent role applies only to design and build contracts.

In a nutshell, within a design and build contract, there's an obligation for a third-party employer's agent to protect the client. This is necessary because, by the very nature of a design and build contract, the client isn't employing a separate architect and other consultants - it's all being done by the building contractor firm. The employer's agent role is therefore designed to mitigate the risk and help protect the client, essentially because the client is putting all their eggs in one basket.

Some of the key employer's agent duties include:

- Confirming the design work to be carried out by the design and build contractor.
- Confirming which approvals are required before construction can start.
- Arranging for signature of the contract and checking the contractor's insurance.
- Reviewing the design in line with planning consent and client requirements.

- Monitoring progress on site and holding regular progress meetings.
- Certifying completion and organising the snagging lists.

PRO TIP

The contract administrator and employer's agent may look very similar on paper, but they operate in different ways – one is a neutral party, while the other works solely on behalf of the employer (you). Therefore, you wouldn't have one person acting in both of these roles. You would either work with an employer's agent (specifically on design and build contracts) or a contract administrator (on other construction contracts).

Some building contractors may offer their own in house project management service, but be aware that these individuals will not be acting independently. They may, in some instances, claim to be acting on behalf of both parties, but a project manager that's employed by the contractor is ostensibly just another member of the contractor's staff and should be considered accordingly.

To keep things simple, I use project manager (PM) as a catch-all umbrella term throughout this book, even though certain tasks may fall under contract administration, or you may be working with an employer's agent.

PRO TIP

A good first step is to talk to a project management firm to see which particular route might be best for your project, if you can get a personal referral then even better! And always, always ensure your chosen project management firm has professional indemnity insurance to cover their actions in the case of negligence, and that the value of cover is adequate for your scheme.

Other roles to consider

There are some other important roles that may or may not fall under the services offered by your project management firm (depending on the firm's size and expertise). These are:

- Quantity surveyor (QS). Many project management firms will have their own QS service in house (mine does). The QS will usually be involved in the initial feasibility estimates and procurement/ tender process, and will later work to keep an eye on costs and cash flow during the construction phase. You may even instruct the QS to manage the development budget so that all costs are recorded, reconciled and certified for payment (including those of other consultants, statutory fees, reports, etc.). Choosing a firm with an in-house QS ensures you get that service right the way through your project.
- Principle designer. This role is a legal requirement under the CDM Regulations mentioned previously, which affect the health and safety practice for the design, build and operation of a building. If your project management firm doesn't offer a principal designer service, the role is often carried out by the architect or contractor. You should be aware that for all commercial developments, regardless of size, the law considers the employer (again, that's you!) to be the principal designer, unless you clearly discharge this obligation to a third party beforehand.

WHY NOT JUST GO DOWN THE 'DESIGN AND BUILD' ROUTE?

You may be wondering why I don't just simplify this pre-construction phase by choosing a design and build contractor. Let me delve into my reasoning.

The pros and cons

Many big contractor firms will have their own in-house architecture offering, which means they can tout for 'design and build' contracts. Now, this seems like a great option for beginner developers because you don't need to faff around hiring a separate architect and various other consultants. The contractor handles it all for you – all those niggly pre-construction tasks and the construction itself. Sounds great, right?

It's certainly attractive, but it can be a very costly way of developing. For one thing, the contractor is taking on a lot of risk, particularly when it comes to the design aspect. And this means they'll be building a healthy buffer into their fee to cover that risk.

What's more, it may not be the most efficient way of going about things. With design and build, you're setting out the ultimate destination, but not specifying how you want the builder to get there. How they get from A to B is entirely open to interpretation, and this may not leave you with the best design. Or, the design may not be workable in practice.

In my education and mentoring work, I've heard horror stories of clients paying for a design and build service and ending up with a great-looking design, but it can't physically be built because it doesn't adhere to certain regulations (fire regs, for instance). What seems easy up front can cause delays and problems further down the line.

PRO TIP

In general, for mid-to-large development projects, I recommend separating out the design and build elements and parcelling them out to different specialists. I believe this route allows for greater innovation and a better design overall. Plus, it often works out cheaper because you're not paying one firm to assume all the risk on the project.

My favoured approach

In practice, separating out the design and build elements means:

- At the design stage, you contract with various different specialists, such as an architect, M&E engineer, structural engineer, quantity surveyor, planning consultant, and so on - essentially, all the services needed to achieve a design and planning approval. (Circle back to Chapter 3 for a list of the various consultants who might be involved in a typical property development lifecycle.) The consultant appointment documents for these individual services will be informed by the governing body associated with that field, for example, RICS for quantity surveyors, RIBA for architects, etc.
- Then, you appoint a contractor to take on the build. (I talk about the different types of building contracts later in the chapter.)

If this seems like more work, it is! But remember, your PM will be doing this for you. Another reason why hiring a PM is money well spent.

PRO TIP

At the design stage, keep in mind that experts have a tendency to over-engineer solutions, particularly when it comes to the architect's drawings and M&E drawings. I get that they do this to reduce their own professional risk, but it can seriously push up build costs. Plus, you may end up with a solution that goes way beyond what you actually need. Think critically at each stage about what the building really needs and seek a second opinion where necessary – your PM and QS will be able to help with this.

THE DESIGN PROCESS

The bigger the development, the more detailed the design drawings get, so this stage will vary greatly depending on your project. According to the RIBA Plan of Work (which lists all the tasks and outputs required at each key stage of a construction project), there are five stages associated with planning and design:

- 0: Strategic Definition - this strategic appraisal phase is about determining the best way of achieving the client's requirements.
- 1: Preparation and Briefing - which involves preparing a detailed project brief.
- 2: Concept Design - here, the architectural concept is created, including key engineering requirements.
- 3: Spatial Coordination - in which the architectural and engineering information is turned into a spatially coordinated design.
- 4: Technical Design - then comes all the technical design information needed to actually construct the project.

Obviously, the RIBA Plan of Work is designed for architects to follow, so if it seems rather complex, don't worry. On my mid-to-large developments, I find it easier to think of the design process as two phases:

- First, you will need some basic design drawings to satisfy the planning process, typically GA (General Arrangement) floorplans, elevation drawings and site (location) plans. Exact requirements may depend on what you are proposing to do and what planning route applies - see Chapter 6.
- Then you will need more detailed design drawings to a) satisfy building control and b) give the builders something to work from. Even if you've had builders do a quick site assessment and give an estimate of costs, they'll still need to do a full quote based on drawings. Note that these detailed design drawings can take several weeks to complete.

'Building control' refers to the building regulations that apply to most building works. These regulations set minimum standards for the design, construction and alteration of buildings – which means designs and works are subject to inspection and approval. (Note that building control approval is entirely separate from planning approval, and usually comes after the planning process.)

In a nutshell, building control approval is all about ensuring that what you build is structurally sound, with all the measures for the protection of life being compliant and legal. Think of building control as being a bit like a police officer overseeing certain key elements of the project, but from a building regs point of view. You'll need building control signoff on your designs, plus building control will want to visit the site during the construction phase (see Chapter 8).

PRO TIP

My advice is to provide detailed design drawings to satisfy building control as soon as possible. You should ask the approved inspector to 'plan check' your initial scheme (for which they will charge a fee). After all, what's the point of designing a layout only to find out later it doesn't comply with the approved inspector's requirements and therefore can't be constructed? I would recommend you secure plan check approval prior to going out to tender. That way, the builder's price is more reliable, because you know it will not need to be changed to satisfy the inspector at a later date. (Invariably, after you've appointed a builder, he may not be quite as competitive with his prices as he was during the tender period, so the cost of additional changes to satisfy building control can quickly add up.)

Your PM will agree the design brief with you, brief the architect and other design consultants on your behalf, and liaise with building control for signoff on the designs.

THE TENDERING PROCESS – GETTING QUOTES FROM BUILDERS

Also known as procurement, this process of seeking and comparing quotes from different contractors is a crucial part of the pre-construction stage. This is where you turn the ballpark figures you had in mind when first weighing up the project (head back to Chapter 5 for more on sourcing and assessing development opportunities) into clearer numbers. Of course, it's not just about assessing prices – you'll also be assessing the different contractor's proposed schedules.

A good PM will have their own 'black book' of preferred contractors – people they trust and have worked with successfully in the past. You may also bring your own list of contractors you'd like to tender for the project.

PRO TIP

If you're unfamiliar with a particular builder, even if your PM vouches for them, I'd always recommend doing your own due diligence on them. As a minimum, this means checking out reviews and asking to see previous jobs.

The importance of accuracy

Personally, I think separating out the design and build elements leads to better, more accurate tenders for the building work. If your team has done a good job on the design, you should find that the various different building quotes are pretty close on price. But you should still assess each one carefully.

Again, an experienced PM is worth their weight in gold when assessing different proposals, particularly when it comes to comparing prices and schedules on a like-for-like basis. As an example, I once had a range of quotes from several contractors and one of the quotes was almost £100k cheaper than the others – plus, the schedule was shorter. My eagle-eyed PM spotted that the contractor had missed something not immediately obvious off the quote, which made his price and schedule look artificially much more attractive. It wasn't a fair comparison, in other words, and had I jumped in with the cheaper contractor, thinking I was saving myself loads of time and money, there would have been trouble further down the line.

As mentioned, the project management firm that I use also includes quantity surveyors. At tender stage, the QS is there to check that the quantities and prices included in quotes are appropriate and reasonable – and, after reviewing the quotes, make a recommendation as to which contractor offers the best value.

Is fixed-price the way to go?

I do a lot of mentoring and one of the questions I get asked frequently is, 'Should I ask for fixed-price quotes?' The short answer is yes, wherever possible. Fixed-price quotes are obviously more desirable, and I'd always expect to agree a fixed price on big projects, where the risk is higher. But it's important to note that, even in a fixed-price quote, certain prices will be provisional – essentially these are estimate prices only, where firm numbers aren't yet available. Glazing is a good example of a provisional cost.

Provisional costs are most likely to be included when the level of detail provided to the contractor at tender stage is simply not enough for them to price the work accurately. As provisional prices can go up as well as down, any tendering contractor may underestimate the values in the bid in order for it to seem more attractive. However, when actual surveys on site are carried out, the reality may be somewhat different, and the costs will vary accordingly. Expenditure of the provisional sum is instructed by the PM and should clearly show any 'add or omit' values (more on this in Chapter 8) for reconciliation at the final account stage. Don't forget to clarify whether provisional sums listed are inclusive or exclusive of the contractor's overheads and profit.

PRO TIP

Even on a fixed-price project, certain costings won't become concrete until the project is underway. With a good team on board, particularly with a good QS, the costs should be predictable and in line with expectations.

The below graph demonstrates cost accuracy vs time. As you can see the further on the project progresses the more accurate the estimation of the final cost will be as there are less unknowns. Of course, once you're finished the build and the final account done then you have 100% accuracy!

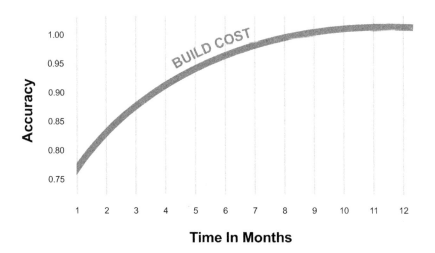

I talk more about managing costs and cash flow in Chapter 8.

Negotiating on prices

You may want to try and negotiate some prices down at the tendering stage. This doesn't just apply to the overall price for the whole project – you may want to drill down to specific elements of the job. For example, say most of the contractor quotes allow £30,000 for carpentry costs, but your favoured contractor's quote allows £35,000 for carpentry. You could ask them to bring the carpentry costs down in line with other comparable quotes. (You can always ask. They don't have to agree!).

PRO TIP

Don't forget to allow for the payment of VAT, which, depending on the type of build, could be rated between zero and 20% (at the time of writing). While you may be able to recover the tax if you are VAT registered, you still need to allow for such funds.

Keeping funder requirements in mind

If you're funding the development with money from a lender, it's very possible they may want to be involved with the tender process. The lender may, for example, want to see your tender documents before you go out to tender, or see quotes before you appoint the contractor. This can seem like a pain in the butt, and it can even delay the start of the project, but it's really important to keep your funder happy at all stages of the project. I talk more about funder requirements in Chapter 8.

CONTRACTING WITH YOUR BUILDER

By this point, you and your PM have been through the tender process. You've assessed the different quotes and decided who you're going to work with. Now comes the contract stuff . . .

Issuing a letter of intent

Prior to signing a formal contract with your contractor, it may be wise to issue a letter of intent. This applies when you want the builder to get on with certain tasks before you've got approval on the design (therefore, you aren't yet ready to sign a full contract for the build). Say, for example, if you want the contractor to get on and secure the site, or make the building watertight, or get started on stripping out the site, you can sign a letter of intent covering just those services. Think of a letter of intent as a mini-pre-contract for specific jobs, before you proceed to the main building contract.

This letter of intent should have a maximum expenditure value stipulated. It should also set out the scope of the minimal activities required and make reference to the main contract itself, which would probably still be in preparation. Other key conditions to note are insurance, valuation and payment dates. Most importantly, though, the letter of intent should establish the length of time you can delay before issuing the full contract, whilst still maintaining the agreed contract sum and works programme period.

JCT contracts

Let's now assume you're ready to progress to the full contract. Unless the project is pretty small, you'll generally be working with a principal or main contractor. And this means you'll contract directly with them, rather than signing separate agreements with every single sub-contractor who sets foot on site. The contractor will take care of appointing all the various trades, in other words. Under the CDM Regulations mentioned previously, the principal contractor will also be solely in charge of the site, and wholly responsible for who visits and allowing them on site.

PRO TIP

Construction contracts are there to protect both parties. Not only does the contract set out the contractor's duties, it will also set out what happens in the event of problems during (and even after) the construction. Don't ever be tempted to settle for a handshake agreement, even if you've worked with the builder before.

You'll typically sign a JCT (Joint Contracts Tribunal) contract with your building contractor. Created in 1931 by RIBA, the JCT is the UK's most widely recognised provider of construction contracts. I wouldn't sign anything else.

There is a range of JCT contracts to choose from including a Minor Works Building Contract, Intermediate Building Contract, and Major Project Construction Contract. The difference between them isn't necessarily about the value of the project, more it's about the level of risk involved. Your PM will be able to advise you on which is most appropriate for your project, but my firm generally uses the intermediate contract.

As well as minor, intermediate and major building contracts, the JCT also provides design and build contracts, plus repair and maintenance, and even project management contracts.

Other key points to note about construction contracts

One of the main ways a contract protects you is by setting out what happens in the event of a problem or breach of contract. This is in no way an exhaustive list, but the main clauses to pay attention to here are.

- Your contract must include some provision for 'latent defects', where you can legally bring a claim for breach of contract after the build is finished. Latent defects are defects that exist at the time of construction but go unnoticed until after the construction is finished, potentially years after completion. (An example might be a steel beam that is the correct specified size but isn't strong enough.) There will be a time limit written into the contract on when you can bring action against the contractor for breach of contract – six years if the contract is signed 'under hand' (i.e. signed only by the parties or their representatives), or 12 years if it is executed 'under deed' (i.e. signed and executed in the presence of a formal witness). Those periods run from the date of practical completion.
- Your contract must also cover 'liquidated and ascertained damages' (LADs for short). LADs are predetermined damages agreed between the parties before the contract is finalised, allowing an injured party to collect compensation in the event of a specific breach of contract – usually, in the case of construction, a culpable delay (i.e. a delay that is the fault of the contractor). So, basically, if your builder is late and it's entirely their fault, they have to pay a penalty or provide a discount.
- Collateral warranties are often used to support a main building contract, where an agreement is needed with a third party outside of the main contract (sub-contractors working for the main contractor, for instance). These set out obligations on the sub-contractor to, for example, use materials of a certain quality or carry out the work in a professional manner. While you probably won't need collateral warranties for all sub-contractor work, it's certainly a useful thing to have on big-ticket items (steel, roofing, windows, etc.) because

it gives you a direct contractual relationship with those providers. So, should the main contractor go bust, you have some recourse in the event of defects related to sub-contractor work. These warranties also form part of the suite of JCT contracts and are often a pre-requisite to lending by some funders.

PRO TIP

Another useful clause in construction contracts is what's known as the 'contractor's design portion'. This is where you're presenting the contractor with a finished design, but you're allowing the builder to come up with design alternatives, where appropriate. Essentially, you're saying, 'Hey, if you can come up with a better, cheaper way of doing this, we're all ears!'

CASE STUDY: HAMPSHIRE CONVERSION

The project

Conversion of a 30,000 square foot office building into more than 40 flats.

The details

On this project, I was advising one of my acquisition mentorship clients. (Acquisition mentorship meaning I bring my development expertise to a client's project, taking the lead on finding a suitable site, bringing in the finance team and solicitors, employing the project management team, implementing the design and more. It's a service designed for less experienced developers or developers who simply want to be more hands-off with their projects.)

So, I pulled the team together, starting of course with my go-to project management team. The PM then appointed specialist design consultants in order of priority for this particular site. In this case, some of the early (and not necessarily obvious) priorities included:

- We had to get a drainage consultant to assess the site - largely because we needed to know at design stage whether the existing drainage (which was designed to service just a few toilets per floor) could cope with the 40+ bathrooms that would be installed. In this case it was fine, but paying for this assessment up front reduced our costs and risk further down the line.
- Because the building was being converted into flats, we also hired a consultant to do an acoustic assessment - basically, sound and vibration tests - to see whether the design needed special acoustic flooring. As it turned out, acoustic flooring was needed, but at least we knew early in the project.
- Fire strategy is also critical to the overall design of flats. In this particular office building, there were lots of exits and six internal staircases. We needed to know whether we could demolish some of these internal staircases (which would make space for more flats) and still comply with fire regulations. Thanks to the fire consultant's assessment, we determined that we could safely demolish three out of the six staircases.

Something like fire strategy may not sound like a big deal, but in this case it was fundamental to the number of flats we could fit in the building, and the layout of those flats. A design with three internal staircases (instead of the existing six) meant we could build more flats - which made a significant difference to the bottom line.

Had we simply appointed a design and build contractor for this project, the contractor might have assumed the worst on all these elements (for example, that the drainage would need to be upgraded, or that we needed to retain all six staircases), in order to reduce their risk. By doing this extra design grunt work, we were able to achieve the most efficient design possible - and, in turn, brief potential building contractors with much more accuracy. By our estimates, this easily saved us 10% on the total project costs.

The key takeaway

This build worked out cheaper in the long run because we contracted out the design work separately to the building work. Doing this reduces risk for the building contractor, thereby bringing down the build costs.

CHAPTER 8

NAVIGATING THE CONSTRUCTION AND POST-CONSTRUCTION PHASES

By this stage, the design work is completed, you've done all the upfront grunt work that is necessary for construction to start. And you've appointed a contractor. Now you're ready to tackle the construction and, in turn, post-construction phases. This chapter sets out the key considerations for these phases.

A few things to note before we get started:

- Once again, I'm working on the assumption that you'll be partnering with an independent project manager (PM). (Circle back to Chapter 7 if you still need convincing of the value a professional project manager will bring to your development projects.)
- Remember that I'm using PM as a catch-all phrase here, when in fact the tasks described may be carried out by a contract administrator or employer's agent. (More on this back in Chapter 7.)
- What follows isn't an exhaustive list of how to project manage a build. Rather, this is what you need to know from the client's

perspective. This is important because, even though your PM will handle the nitty gritty oversight of the project, you as the client will still need to be involved.

- Finally, because each development project is different, not all of the considerations mentioned will apply to every single one of your developments. Most of it is applicable to medium-sized developments and upwards, but even then there will be variations.

MANAGING FUNDER REQUIREMENTS

I could easily have titled this section 'Keeping your funder sweet,' which is an important consideration to understand as a property developer.

When you first start out in property development, you may be funding your projects with a straightforward mortgage or even a personal loan. But as you progress to larger projects, it's much more likely you'll need specific development finance. (Circle back to Chapter 4 for more on how development finance works, plus alternative funding options.) When you work with a lender in this way (be it a bank or a specialist lender), they will quite rightly want to monitor your project closely to protect their investment.

In practice, this means the lender's representative – usually a quantity surveyor (QS), although they may be called a 'fund monitor' in this context – will visit your site once a month or so to value the work that's been done and ensure that the lender's money is being spent wisely.

These site visits are necessary because lenders release their funding in stages, or tranches, with each drawdown (payment) only being released at certain milestones. If the lender isn't happy with the work being done or if the project is behind schedule, they may refuse to release the next drawdown.

As you can imagine, this process can have a huge knock-on effect in terms of cash flow (which I cover next). It obviously affects the amount of money you have in the bank at any one time, and how (and when) you pay your contractor. Depending on your lender, they may want to approve the contractor's invoices before releasing funding – and given that most building contracts require regular contractor payments, this can involve quite a bit of admin.

Under a JCT contract (see Chapter 7), the PM must ensure that the QS and contractor carry out a valuation at the agreed intervals (normally monthly or every four weeks). Then, once the contractor has submitted an 'application for payment' (basically, an invoice) – ideally having agreed the amount beforehand with your QS – a 'payment certificate' is issued by the QS. You as the client then pay this value on the payment certificate (and not the builder's invoice value, if it happens to be different). Submission of the payment application by the builder must be made by the scheduled date, as must the issue of the payment certificate by the QS. You then need to pay within the period of time stipulated in the main contract.

You can see how there are quite a few admin stages before the contractor gets paid. It's really important that the funder isn't allowed to delay this process, otherwise you as the client may find yourself in breach of contract for late payment. It's therefore crucial that you agree beforehand with your funder what their documented requirements will be every month. Your PM should be able to ensure this information is collated in a timely manner.

PRO TIP

It's important to keep your funder happy, even if their oversight feels (at times) like a burden you could really do without.

Clearly all this only applies when you're working with a lender. You may have gone down a more creative finance route and funded your development through a joint venture agreement with a partner. In this case, your joint venture partner may want to carry out their own checks on site (or appoint their own QS to do this), which is absolutely fine, but there's certainly no obligation or expectation for them to do so. In my experience, having a JV partner monitor the build separately isn't that common. If you think about it, you're both technically the same client.

MANAGING CASH FLOW

Too many projects fail or are jeopardised because of cash flow problems. And this becomes more of a risk the bigger your project.

I've seen so many developers end up in the awful catch 22 situation of not having cash in the bank to pay the builders, which means the builders stop work, yet the lender won't pay out the next payment until the builders complete the next milestone. See what I mean about catch 22? The bank won't cough up until the next stage of the build is completed, yet the builders won't come back to work until you pay them what you owe.

Therefore, the success of a development project isn't just about keeping a beady eye on your costs. Nor is it about having a healthy contingency buffer (although you should obviously have a contingency on each project – 10% of the total cost being a good rule of thumb). No doubt cost management and contingency are important. But equally important is understanding your project's cash flow.

In basic terms, this means:

- Knowing exactly when the contractor expects to be paid (which should be clearly set out in their quote and the contract) – particularly when big-ticket items, such as windows, need to be paid for.
- Knowing when you expect to receive payments from your lender.
- Making sure you get your drawdown payments in good time to pay the contractor. (If not, you'll be paying them out of your own pocket if you don't want them to stop work.)

It's incredibly easy to get this wrong. Your PM and QS will take the lead on the day-to-day cash flow oversight, and will usually use a specific cash flow management tool for the job. But you'll be the one receiving and making payments, so it's really important you understand what is expected of you and when.

The JCT contract allows the client to retain a nominal amount of money each valuation (normally 5%), which accrues month by month until the project reaches 'practical completion' – at which time, half of that accrued amount (2.5%) is released to the contractor. The remaining balance is retained by the client, and then usually on the 12-month anniversary of reaching practical completion, the balance is paid to the contractor (assuming no further defects are evident). This retention can be helpful for cash flow planning but don't forget that you eventually have to pay it, so make sure you set it aside in advance.

You should ask your QS to provide you with an indicative cash flow at the beginning of the project, and this could include all the associated consultant stage payments and other miscellaneous costs if the QS is maintaining the development budget. Your funder may also wish to see this forecast for their own planning purposes.

It is also critical you see a copy of the contractor's cash flow for the project, as it may illustrate why you have the most expensive hole in the ground but cheapest roof! The contractor will invariably hope to secure as much money as soon as possible so may price a project with expensive initial ground works and cheaper roof works. These costs will not be the true cost of the specific activity, but a means for the builder to secure maximum early funding. If this is the case with your contractor, be very cautious; if the contractor was to disappear for any reason, you may find you've paid, say, 60% of the value for only 30% of the actual work. A good QS will ensure this situation doesn't occur, but history is littered with naïve clients who have paid hefty upfront deposits, only to find their friendly builder has suddenly vanished with the money or has used it to fund other ventures.

As a side note, cash flow is also a good way to indicate whether a project is on time or not. If the contractor has failed to claim all the money he forecast he would require by a certain date, chances are that is because he hasn't actually done the work yet so either his works programme needs revising or the cash flow forecast does.

PRO TIP

When your cash flow is especially healthy, you may be able to negotiate some nifty discounts by offering to pay on fast terms. As an example, I once negotiated a discount of almost £30,000 on a project by agreeing to pay the builder within seven days. Obviously, this can be a risky approach, so is only worth considering when you're absolutely sure your cash flow can support such a strategy and the builder can be relied upon to behave appropriately.

MANAGING THE BUILD COSTS

This falls under the remit of the PM and, more importantly, the QS.

The QS should be one of the consultants brought on board during the pre-construction phase, to help with assessing designs and tenders. (You may even work with a QS when assessing potential development projects, if you're not confident ballparking costs yourself.) Ideally, your PM firm will have this QS service in house – I've certainly found that to be beneficial on my projects.

During the construction phase, the QS is working to:

- Keep an eye on costs.
- Make sure any provisional numbers in the quote become firm numbers as soon as possible.

- Remeasure certain work activities if necessary, to ensure that the builder's claim is based on the correct quantity and at the appropriate rate.
- Generally balance costs and specifications (for example, choosing higher/lower specification materials as you go through the build).

'Value engineering' is another term you might hear associated with the QS's role. This essentially means reducing your costs as you go along, and finding ways to save money as the build progresses (though, normally, a value engineering meeting is carried out involving all parties prior to agreeing the main contract value).

PRO TIP

I'm a big fan of value engineering (as you might guess)! However, not all contractors are open to the value engineering approach. It's therefore important to find a contractor who is open to keeping costs down and helping the QS find items to save money on. If you think about it, value engineering works in the contractor's favour, since you're more likely to work with them on future projects if they've been open to reducing costs where reasonable.

In other words, with a good QS on board, your build costs should ideally come down as the build progresses, not go up. And if you do find that costs are going up, the QS will shop around to bring those costs back down.

If I'm honest, it took me a bit of time to get used to the idea of paying a QS to assume this role for me. On my early projects I would manage costs myself, but it definitely wasn't the most efficient approach, especially given that I wanted to scale up my property business. Having the QS (in conjunction with the PM) manage this aspect for me has ultimately paid dividends. Now, my projects get built better and most cost effectively.

MANAGING THE BUILD PROGRAMME

Whenever contractors or PMs talk about 'programming' or 'the programme', they're referring to the works schedule. The contractor and PM will collaborate closely on this aspect of the build – everything from planning works and creating a detailed schedule to booking contractors at the appropriate stages.

You should absolutely be given a detailed programme for your project. (When tendering for the project, the contractor will have given you a schedule of works, but it won't be as detailed as the programme you see at construction phase.) The programme you see at this stage should look like a Gantt chart, listing all the trades required on the project (plasterer, windows, roofing, etc), with timings for each. It's often created using specialist project management software, such as Microsoft Projects.

While some trades will overlap, there's generally a natural progression to any project, where certain trades have to follow other trades. There's a fine line between having enough people on site at the same time to keep the project moving efficiently, and having so many people on site they're getting in each other's way and slowing things down. Then there's the knock-on effect of any delays – meaning, if one trade moves back, the rest have to move back accordingly. Getting all the various trades lined up in the right order, planning who's coming in when, and what's being fitted when, is akin to herding cats, so be grateful this falls to the contractor and PM!

You may be advised that 'critical path analysis' of the programme has identified a certain problem or pending challenge. Simply put, a few activities can have a disproportionate effect on the rest of the build. For instance, if the floor slab isn't complete, you can't begin to construct the internal walls, or if the mains power isn't on, then the testing and commissioning of all the M&E systems cannot be progressed. As the client, you should familiarise yourself with the works programme and try and identify where and when the key works activities take place. By understanding the process better and being able to interpret the works programme, you will be better placed to anticipate and mitigate any problems before they become a significant issue. Again, your PM should already be on top of this and able to advise you further, but it's still a good idea to know your programme.

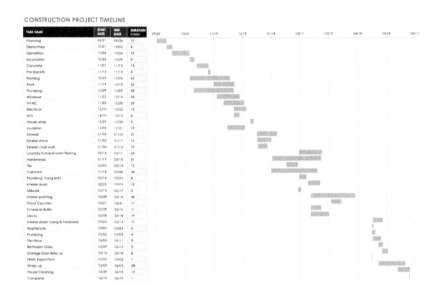

CONSTRUCTION PROJECT TIMELINE

PRO TIP

The contractor is responsible for keeping the programme up to date, and will generally issue an updated version each month. The PM's role here is to monitor these updates, keep an eye on the programme, pick up when things aren't happening on time – and, of course, keep you in the loop on the schedule.

Finally, even on the smoothest project, it's not unusual for timings to shift slightly. When this happens, it's vital the PM communicates the schedule changes to you, and that the affected tradespeople are informed, especially if they are directly employed by you and not part of the main contractor's team (for example, kitchen deliveries, sign writers, landscape gardeners, etc.).

WHAT TO EXPECT IN TERMS OF MONITORING PROGRESS AND PROGRESS REPORTS

One of the PM's key duties during the construction phase is to regularly update you on progress. With my PM, this takes the shape of:

- The PM and I talk maybe three times a week, just so he can quickly update me on how the build is going. On a complex build, we might even talk daily.
- We'll then have a more formal weekly meeting together, where the PM gives me an in-depth progress report. Here, we might go through the programme, discuss any significant changes on the project, and chat through upcoming stages.
- There is also a monthly site meeting, where the whole team involved in the project at that particular stage gets together on site – including the architect, the PM and myself. The purpose of this meeting is to generally review progress, but also to discuss any problems that need troubleshooting and any design changes that may be required. It's vital this meeting is minuted, and that the minutes are circulated to all. Should a dispute ever arise, those minutes can form the basis of a very important set of documents that clearly and concisely record who agreed to do what and when.

No matter how hard you prepare at the pre-construction phase, development projects can throw up unexpected challenges – especially when you're converting or developing an older building.

Say the contractor discovers a problem that means a wall needs to move by a few inches. This could impact other factors, such as the fire strategy, safety regulations, or even the saleability of your end product (for example, if saleable space in a flat is reduced). This is the sort of decision that needs to be discussed at the monthly site meetings, so you can see why you need to be there. It's really important that the client is involved in any design decisions.

Making these decisions at construction phase can be a challenge as a developer. You may need to alter your original design from the optimal end product to satisfy regulations, or simply to solve a problem that's cropped up. Ultimately, it's about finding a balance between your perspective as the developer (someone who is obviously focused on what's right for your chosen exit strategy, see Chapter 2) and what's necessary to push the build ahead. You can't always have what you want, in other words.

Wherever changes do need to be made, the change control process kick in, which brings me to . . .

UNDERSTANDING THE FORMAL CHANGE CONTROL PROCESS

If you've got a few smaller development projects under your belt, particularly if they were projects without lots of detailed design drawings, you may be used to making changes as the build progresses, and simply agreeing the new price with your builder. (Although, even on these smaller projects, I always tried to keep changes at construction phase to a minimum.)

The bigger the project, however, the more detailed the design drawings become. Which means the change control process - 'change control' referring to anything that is a change from the original design drawings - becomes all the more important.

The first thing to say - obvious though it is - is that, by the time you get to construction phase, design changes should be kept to an absolute minimum. No one wants to see the client wandering around site, making off-the-cuff changes just because they feel like it. This pushes up build costs, often causes delays, and most certainly annoys the contractor (not to mention the PM).

But when changes are necessary, there's a formal change control process to follow. And this means you as the client never approach the contractor and ask them to make changes directly.

PRO TIP

Change requests must go through your PM for a formal instruction. This means the PM will work with the contractor (and possibly the QS) to assess the costs associated with the change, sign off the revised costs *before* any work is done, and issue a formal change notice to the contractor documenting the change. This leaves a nice paper trail, thereby reducing the risk of conflicts further down the line.

Even something as small as adding extra plug sockets to a room may mean updating design drawings, and will obviously have an impact in terms of costs (and maybe even the schedule). It's vital the change is recorded as a change notice, and that the builder's total contract sum is amended in line with the change.

The change notice often takes the form of an 'add and omit' notice, which means it records what is being omitted from the design and what is being added in its place. For example, if you're changing the spec of your windows, the change notice might record that you are omitting white windows costing £20,000 (as an example) and adding grey windows at a cost of £25,000. The total contract sum will also be amended to take account of the additional £5,000 cost.

Unless you're a miracle worker, this change control process will kick in on pretty much every project where you're converting or developing an existing building. (Change control is less of an issue on new builds.) Buildings will throw challenges at you, and that's a normal part of being a property developer. The important thing is to respect the proper change control process and always go through your PM.

Finally, don't forget that all changes will have an impact on either cost or time, and the main contractor is naturally entitled to extra time or costs if the change cannot be reasonably incorporated within the agreed contract period. It is therefore essential that, unless it cannot be otherwise avoided, specification and scope changes are kept to the absolute minimum. The more unscrupulous contractors may use these changes to try and claw back lost profit or secure additional programme time when they may already be running late as a result of their own failures.

DEALING WITH PROBLEMS AND DISPUTES

Your contract with the builder will have some provision for dealing with disputes, typically including mediation and breach-of-contract penalties (LADs, see Chapter 7).

LADs

In my experience, LADs only kick in in fairly extreme circumstances, i.e. a major breach of contract. (I've only made a claim for LADs once in my career and unfortunately the contractor went bust so we didn't even end up recovering the money due.)

Should your project not be delivered on time, the JCT contract recognises that this delay may cause you additional costs for late completion. The LADs, which will have been agreed beforehand, are there to reflect those likely losses at a reasonable rate that, if challenged, can be proven. However, the contractor cannot be held responsible for every eventuality, so a series of 'relevant events' are listed within the contract that allow the contractor to claim for extra time (and costs) due to these specific events. A typical example might be late changes to the design by the client or late delivery of the utility supply by either the electric, gas or water company. Of course, these claims for more time have to be qualified and proven, but they do occur.

If, however, the contractor is late without good reason then you are perfectly entitled to apply the LADs at the agreed rate or part thereof. Your QS will provide further details as to how this is done but, in simple terms, an adjustment is made at the final account stage to deduct the LADs from the amount owed.

How to resolve disputes

Most times, a dispute can be resolved quickly and amicably in a frank discussion between the PM, contractor and yourself. I've found that's usually enough to resolve the issue. But if that doesn't work, independent intervention may be appropriate.

Within the JCT contract, the parties are given the option of either going to 'adjudication' or 'arbitration' for the settlement of any disputes. Prior to the signing of the main contract, the parties will agree which route is most appropriate for them. Usually the independent individual responsible for adjudication or arbitration is a specially trained expert from either RICS or other such recognised professional body.

Going to court is considered the nuclear option - it can serve as a useful deterrent, but it's only ever a last resort! If you resort straight to court, the likelihood is the judge will instruct you to follow the agreed measures detailed within the contract. Only if no settlement is reached can the matter then be referred to court. Specialist construction lawyers do not come cheap so it makes sense to follow the path outlined in the contract before resorting to litigation, which can be very expensive and offers no guarantees.

Thankfully, most disputes never get that far. If you've done your due diligence at pre-contract stage, have a solid design, and are working with a reputable contractor, most disputes will be fairly minor and easily resolved. Often the dispute is because something will take longer than planned (which may not even be the contractor's fault).

If you do encounter a problem with your contractor or end up in a dispute, your PM is your first port of call. Remember I mentioned the role of contract administrator back in Chapter 7, and how this involves working in the best interests of both parties to resolve any issues? This is yet another example of how partnering with a professional PM is money well spent.

PRO TIP

Sometimes, the smart move is to concede on an issue, even if the contractor is at fault. As an example, I once had a project where the builder under-quoted something and we later found out it was going to cost more. Rather than get into an expensive legal dispute over who was liable for the extra costs, which would have only served to delay the project, I decided to absorb the extra cost. To me, it was more important to get the site finished and start earning income from it than to prove I was in the right.

In the event that you're really having trouble with a builder and their work isn't up to scratch (which, again, should be rare if you've done your due diligence), your PM will monitor their work carefully for the duration of the build. If things get really bad, you have the option of terminating their contract and bringing in a new builder, but you'll need to comply with the terms and notice period detailed within the contract for termination of their services.

NAVIGATING THE BUILDING CONTROL INSPECTION PROCESS

You can expect your building control inspector to visit the site during construction - usually these visits will be arranged in advance but sometimes the inspector may turn up unannounced on site for a surprise inspection (albeit this is less common).

As mentioned in Chapter 3, it's a good idea to appoint a private, independent approved inspector for your project as opposed to the traditional local authority officer. Chances are you will save money, receive regular reports, develop a relationship with an individual not bound by geographical constraints regarding site locations, and, frankly, have more opportunity to debate and influence the interpretation and application of certain building regulations on your site.

PRO TIP

Your PM will liaise with the building control inspector, but it's well worth making sure your PM takes detailed photos of major structural elements, just so you have that paper trail. In the event that your building control inspector leaves or hasn't taken proper pictures, you have documented the build and can prove it's been built correctly.

TACKLING THE POST-CONSTRUCTION MILESTONES

When you get to the end of the build, there are certain tasks and milestones that need to be completed before the building can be occupied (and in some cases, some jobs may continue even after the building is occupied). This phase is known as 'post-construction'.

The key milestones here are:

- Pre-completion snagging and builder's clean
- Practical completion
- Building control signoff
- Final handover

Let's look at each area in turn.

Pre-completion snagging and builder's clean

Snagging generally breaks down into a couple of stages. First, there is the initial snagging list, which aims to capture every final job that needs doing – such as fixing a door that doesn't close properly.

PRO TIP

On my projects, I have the PM do the initial snagging round, but it can also be contracted out to a third-party snagging company. On larger developments, snagging can be a huge job, so don't be tempted to tackle it yourself. (Personally, I like to go around the site and check the snagging jobs have been completed to a high standard, but I wouldn't dream of compiling the full snagging list myself.)

In general, as a result of this first round of snagging, you're aiming to achieve what's known as 'practical completion' – more on this coming up next.

Then, when the contractor has worked through the initial snagging list, and you've achieved practical completion, there may be a final round of minor snags to complete. For example, maybe the painter needs to come back and fix some scuffs in the paintwork once all the other contractors are off site. Depending on what needs doing, the timings on this final round of snagging can be fairly fluid, and may take place after the contractor has handed over the keys (final handover) and you've taken possession of the site.

Around this time, the site will also undergo a thorough builder's clean. Organised by the main contractor (who will probably sub-contract it out to a specialist firm), this is where all the builder's waste is cleared up and the site is given a deep clean.

Practical completion

Practical completion is a defined term within the main contract – and because achieving it triggers the release of half of the retention payment held and discharges the contractor from his insurance and health and safety obligations on site, contractors are very keen to reach this stage, often before they really have.

It is at the discretion of the PM to determine when practical completion has been reached, but generally it is achieved when you, the client, can take 'beneficial occupation' (meaning the building is capable of being used). In reality, you may still have a creaky door, dripping tap, dodgy light or even some cracking evident, but none of these relatively trivial items are reason enough not to grant practical completion. If, however, there are major problems (for example, the painting and decorating is so poor it requires extensive making good), then clearly this would not allow a reasonable person to take 'beneficial occupation'. Ultimately, though, it's a matter of interpretation.

One thing is certain: under no circumstances should the PM grant practical completion if the building control approved inspector has not issued his/her 'Final Notice' or 'Final Certificate'. Until this has been done, occupation cannot occur. My PM also likes the contractor to have provided all the building operation information, health and safety file and all other relevant paperwork, as required. That's because it is often harder to secure all the necessary paperwork after a builder has left site and been paid.

Note that you may still have some sub-contractors on site sorting out minor snagging issues *after* practical completion. But, essentially, the building is 99.9% finished at this stage and is suitable for use. When you reach this stage, the PM will issue a certificate of practical completion to the contractor (and this certificate may stipulate that there are certain works still to complete).

PRO TIP

The contractor's insurance cover ends at practical completion, so it's vital you have new insurance cover in place immediately upon practical completion. You'll need different cover depending on whether the building is standing vacant or occupied, so always work with a good insurance broker to find the right policy for your projects.

Building control signoff

This is another key milestone in the post-construction phase, although it technically falls around the practical completion stage. Your PM will liaise with your approved inspector to get signoff and the certificate.

Final handover

This is when the owner (you) or operator (which may be a tenant, if you're renting out the building) formally takes control of the building. This may take place during a formal handover meeting and final inspection of the site.

At handover stage, you (or the operator of the building, if it's not you) will be given everything needed to operate the building, which may or may not include:

- Keys and fobs for door entry.
- Building owner's manual (which contains all the information needed for the operation and maintenance of the building - fire systems, heating systems, etc.).
- Building log book (designed to help the building operator operate the building in the most efficient way possible).

- Building user guide (a non-technical guide to help building users (occupants) operate the building's systems).
- Health and safety file (containing essential health and safety information anyone carrying out future works on the building will need to know).
- Equipment test certificates (for example, lift certificate, fire alarm certificate, gas safety certificate, and energy performance certificates (if applicable)).
- All warranties related to the work (including structural warranties and collateral warranties (see Chapter 7)).

What about defects after handover?

Don't forget that your contract will include a 12-month defects liability period, during which time, should any catastrophic defect occur, the builder is required to attend and correct the defect. If he does not, then you should instruct your PM to write and give him seven days' notice to attend, otherwise you will use some of the balance of the retention money still being held to pay for another contractor to fix the problem. (Because the final balance of the retention is usually not due until 12 months after practical completion.)

PRO TIP

Normally, as a building settles, gets used and is subject to the usual changes in temperature, a few cracks will occur. It's worth waiting until the end of the 12-month defects liability period, and then have the contractor revisit the site and make good any identified defects all in one go.

Once any final defects have been fixed, the PM will then issue an 'End of Defects Period Certificate', which in turn will trigger the release of the final retention payment.

CASE STUDY: REDBRICK HOUSE, NEWBURY, BERKSHIRE

The project

Commercial office to residential conversion creating 42 micro-studios.

The details

I tell this tale to show how, even with an experienced team, mistakes get made.

On this project, the architect had designed a sizeable external bike and bin store to satisfy planners – but it turned out this bike and bin store was much bigger than it really needed to be. Four times bigger to be exact. It got missed by everyone: me, my PM, the contractor. At no stage did any of us stop and ask why this external bin and bike store was so huge!

So when we were well into the construction phase, I turned up for the monthly site meeting and saw this huge concrete slab in the car park, ready for the bike and bin store to be built. It was immediately obvious that it was way bigger than necessary – it was the size of a whole parking space.

In this building's location, a parking space can be rented out for as much as £85 per month. Over 20 years – which is how long my company intends to hold this particular building – that adds up to lost revenue of more than £20,000. As errors on a large construction site go, it could have been worse, but it was certainly a lesson learned.

Had we caught this particular error earlier, we could have gone back to planning and got the revised plans approved. But at this stage in the project, going back to planning would have caused too much of a delay. (Plus the concrete slab had already been poured, which represented a sizeable portion of the total cost of the bin and bike store.) So we stuck with the inordinately large bike and bin store, which still stands on the site to this day.

The key takeaway

Expect the unexpected. Even with the best people in place, something (however minor) will go wrong on pretty much every build. (That's not to put you off - it's just the way it is. This is why we build contingencies into our projects, after all.) Providing you catch them early enough, it's possible to make changes like this during the construction process, but you'll need to weigh up the impact on costs and schedule.

CHAPTER 9

BRINGING YOUR STRATEGY TO A SUCCESSFUL CONCLUSION: SELLING OR RENTING YOUR DEVELOPMENT

The exact definition of a successful conclusion will depend on your chosen strategy. It may mean selling houses or flats on your site to individual buyers for the price you want, selling an entire block of flats to an investor buyer, or keeping hold of your finished development and renting it out for an ongoing income. Circle back to Chapter 2 to revisit why you should always develop with particular strategies in mind.

Ultimately, you have the final say on *how* your finished product is marketed, and for how much, but you'll also have to work with estate agents or lettings agents to get the job done.

Part of the reason I wanted to write this book was to give growing developers a better understanding of how to manage the various experts involved in the property lifecycle - and that includes agents. Therefore, this chapter is all about how best to work with agents to achieve your desired outcome.

Note that, for ease, I use the phrases 'end product' or 'finished product' here, which is after all what you've created. You've created a specific product with a particular target audience in mind, whether it's a luxury new build family home, a block of flats, HMO flats, an aparthotel or whatever. Now it's time to bring that product to market.

PRESENTING YOUR FINISHED PRODUCT – DO YOU NEED SHOW HOMES AND FURNISHINGS?

First up, let's address two questions I'm often asked, one relating to sales and the other to rental properties.

Are show homes worth it?

In a word, no. Not usually, anyway. A huge developer like Taylor Wimpey might routinely build show units so they can start selling properties off-plan long before the development is even completed. But this book assumes you're not taking on massive developments at this stage in your career.

Generally, trying to create a show house or flat on small or mid-sized developments just isn't worth it, primarily because it can have a negative impact on your development's schedule. Accelerating one unit on a site to get it finished before the others means you're throwing your whole schedule out of whack. (For example, you'll have plasterers on site doing the show unit while the rest of the build won't be ready for plastering for months.) Essentially, you end up creating a mini-project within a project, which can be a real headache to manage.

What's more, the cost of creating a show home can be pretty steep, and most developers don't like to give away pure profit for no good reason.

Often, it's not even physically possible to create a show home, particularly when it's part of a larger development, like a block of flats. It's very hard to get the services (water, electrics, etc.) switched on to one unit when the rest of the site isn't live yet (because there are still wires hanging out of the walls and ceilings). You'd have to get temporary services put in just to cover that one unit, which can be really expensive. As I said, a developer like Taylor Wimpey that's developing a site with hundreds of homes will do it. But it's almost never worth it on smaller developments.

I guess the exception would be when you're building something like three or four identical houses on a plot of land, where you have the option of fully completing one of them first. But I'd still think carefully about whether this is worth the potential impact on the development's schedule and bottom line.

PRO TIP

If you want to start marketing your product before construction is finished, you can use CGI to create glossy brochures, or create a virtual reality walkthrough. (As an aside, you can also have photographs of a finished property digitally augmented with furniture and artwork.) Plenty of companies specialise in creating these digital options for developers. Obviously this costs money, but it can be a worthwhile investment if you're building multiple units in one development.

Renting furnished vs unfurnished?

While some buyers may be willing to buy off-plan, renters absolutely need to see the finished product before they sign on the dotted line.

So you're unlikely to attract any tenants until the development is fully finished.

(The exception to this might be a large HMO, where you could in theory get one bedroom ready to show to tenants while the other rooms are still getting their finishing touches. But you wouldn't want to be showing prospective tenants around the site any earlier than that.)

The question most investors want to know about getting rental properties ready for market is: is it worth furnishing rental properties? The answer, like everything else, depends on your rental strategy and target audience.

If you're renting to students, for example, they won't have accumulated the furniture and homewares that older renters might come with, so they'll almost always expect accommodation to come fully furnished.

For professional tenants, it can vary. If it's a short-term let (for example, serviced accommodation apartments aimed at professionals who are in the area on short-term contracts) then it should obviously be furnished. Long-term lets, whether it's a whole flat/house or HMO bedrooms, can go either way. In the case of HMO properties, I'll usually furnish them myself, typically with sturdy built-in furniture such as beds, wardrobes, shelving and bedside units, and factor this into the rental price. If I'm renting a whole flat or house to an individual tenant, couple or family, then I may offer it unfurnished but have furniture in the property for viewings.

PRO TIP

You'll need to do your homework and talk to local agents to determine what the local market and your target demographic expects. But you can always advertise a property as furnished (or part-furnished) with the option of tenants taking it unfurnished if that's what they prefer.

WORKING WITH AN ESTATE AGENT TO SELL YOUR END PRODUCT

When it comes to choosing an estate agent to sell my properties, I don't mess around - I'll happily get every agent in town to view and assess my developments. I recommend you do the same so you can get a broad range of perspectives. Over time, you'll probably develop closer relationships with some agents more than others, and that's great, but I'd still get a wide range of assessments before signing up with a particular agent.

So how can you decide which agent is right, and how should you work with them? Let's start with one of the biggest promises estate agents make: the price they can achieve for your property.

Pricing for the market

As I said at the start of this chapter, you're the customer, so you have the final say on how much you sell your product for. Of course, you should be guided by what agents say and make the most of their knowledge, but in the end, it's you who has to decide the value of your product and how much you are ultimately happy to sell for.

Agents want your business, so there's an obvious temptation for them to inflate the price just so you sign on with them. But pricing too high only puts buyers off, and if your property sits on the market for months it begins to look stale - buyers will wonder why it's still on the market and what's wrong with it. In other words, don't get greedy and be seduced by promises of high prices. Tell agents you want their honest view.

Of course, the price you set isn't just about value. Time is a factor. You can price more cheaply if you want to sell quickly, or if you're comfortable waiting six months to sell your product, you can maybe afford to hold out for a higher price.

When you're selling multiple units in one development - 10 flats, for example - and the market is fairly buoyant, you could always adopt a phased sales approach.

In this approach:

- You release the half of the units (in this example, five flats) for sale at a cheaper price, but hold back the remaining flats.
- The first batch of properties are marketed with a promise that the prices will be going up by, say, 5% when the second batch of flats are released. So if buyers don't commit now, they miss out on a cheaper price.
- Then you release the second batch at the higher price a few months later.
- The first batch of buyers are happy because a) they got a good deal and b) they've earned quick capital growth because the value of their property has gone up so soon after buying. And you're happy because you're closing sales.

You obviously need a reasonably sized development for this to work - I wouldn't bother on anything less than 10 or 15 flats. And there's no reason why you have to stick to a two-phase approach. You could do it in three phases if the size of the development warrants it.

PRO TIP

You might also want to look at any government schemes that are relevant to your development, such as the Help to Buy: Shared Ownership scheme.

Picking the right agent

Having talked to several agents, how do you decide who to sign with? Well, you shouldn't just decide based on price (remember, you dictate the price). You should decide based on which agent offers you the best marketing value.

Good questions to ask in your conversations with agents include:

- How much marketing will you do?
- Will you commit to a certain marketing budget? If so, how much?
- What is your track record in sales?
- Have you sold similar developments to this? When? How much for?

Sometimes you'll get better value from a smaller agent than a big one. A large firm may not value your custom that much, whereas a smaller agent might bend over backwards for you. Sometimes it pays to be a big fish in a small agent's pond!

There's another basic but important factor to consider when weighing up agents: do you get on with them? People like to do business with people they like, so who do you feel you can work best with?

In fact, you don't have to limit yourself to one agent - if you like, you can sign up with two agents on a dual-agency agreement (where both agents market the property and split the fee, so they both get paid, regardless of whoever secures the sale). There are pros and cons to this approach.

One of the biggest downsides is that you have two agents to manage, which can be a bit of a headache. They may disagree on how to market the property and you're left playing piggy in the middle. And they may not be as motivated to sell your property because they're not earning a full fee.

On the plus side, partnering with more than one agent can work really well if you're targeting a niche type of buyer. For example, there are agents out there who market directly to investor buyers rather than owner-occupier buyers. These investor buyers could be buy-to-let individuals, huge property funds and anything in between. A local estate agent might attract some investor buyers (especially local buy-to-let landlords) as well as owner-occupier buyers, but they may struggle to attract larger investors. So, if your development is of a decent size and you want to target investors, you could potentially sign on with a local agent *and* an investment agency with a wider reach.

Working with your estate agent

Having chosen your agent (or agents), you'll need to sign a contract with them.

Make sure you put the agent on a fixed-term contract, where they have exclusivity for a set period of time only (anywhere between one and three months is a good start). If they're not performing, you can cut them loose after this time and try another agent.

PRO TIP

Do feel free to set targets for agents, such as how many viewings you expect to see in the first week or how many units you want sold in the first month. Estate agents are salespeople after all, so set them sales targets. Whether you set sales targets or not, it's really important to be clear about what you expect from your agent. And if they're not cutting the mustard, move on as soon as you can.

WORKING WITH A LETTINGS AGENT

Some of the same considerations will apply here, such as deciding who you'll work best with and clarifying what you expect of them. But there are some specifics to consider for rentals.

Pricing

Again, you have the final say on this, and you'll no doubt have thought about your intended rental price when initially weighing up the development project. Naturally, you'll want to keep your rent competitive in relation to the local market, as renters (just like buyers) are driven away by overcharging.

When talking to agents, you'll also need to discuss whether you should be charging an all-inclusive rent (where all utility bills are included, and the cost of this is factored into the rent), or having the tenants cover the bills themselves. In my experience, tenants tend to prefer the simplicity of an all-inclusive rent, especially on HMO properties (because having to divvy up the bills with their fellow HMO residents, when there can be many people sharing the property, only makes tenants' life harder and the property less desirable). On a single let, where you're renting a whole flat or house (as opposed to bedrooms), you could go either way. Talk to your agent about the best approach for your target audience.

Deciding which type of letting service you need

Different lettings agents offer different levels of service, so you'll need to decide how much work you want to do as a landlord. You can get the agent to do as much or as little as you want, depending on your skills and interests. Some people really enjoy the business of finding and managing tenants, while others want to be as hands-off as possible.

The services offered by lettings agents generally fall into three categories:

- Full lettings and management. With this service, the agent finds and manages all the dealings with tenants, manages the ongoing maintenance of the property and liaises with any tradespeople.
- Let only. Here, the agent will market your property on all the relevant portals, show tenants around, and (if you want) vet tenants and sort out the contract. Then they hand the tenant over to you, and you take on the tenant relationship and property management from there.
- Management only. This is where you find your own tenants and handle the contract, then the agent takes over the ongoing management of the property. This service option is rare, and, to be honest, I've

never really understood who it's designed for. If a landlord is confident marketing a property and engaging tenants, I don't see why they wouldn't be happy to deal with tenants on an ongoing basis?

PRO TIP

With many agents, you can negotiate any level of service you want, and a fee that suits your requirements, based on how much or how little you want to get involved.

Of course, the other option is doing all of this yourself. The ins and outs of marketing and managing rental properties is way beyond the scope of this book but let me say this: doing it all yourself obviously leaves more profit in your pocket, but you'll miss out on the agent's valuable expertise and network. This can be particularly important if you don't have an existing network of tradespeople (plumber, electrician, etc.) you can call up to fix problems at the drop of a hat. Certainly if you're new to an area, I'd recommend working with an agent until you've built up your own network of local, reliable tradespeople.

At this stage of my career, I've built my own in-house team who can handle the rentals side of things for me. These days, I tend to partner with agents on a let-only basis, and use them to do all my rental viewings (which can be time-consuming and really boring, so outsourcing this to an agent is great value). My team then takes over to vet potential tenants, issue the rental agreement, manage the property's maintenance and deal with any tenant problems. This gives me a nice balance of maximising my profit, while still remaining fairly hands off.

A couple of things to consider in the agent's contract

My biggest tip here is to be wary of hidden agents' fees - for example, where the agent adds a 20% margin on top of any repair bills for their own trouble. Crazy lettings fees aren't as bad as they used to be, and of course I don't begrudge lettings agents making a fair living, but you should always make sure you understand what you're signing up for. Check out all the fees fully and make sure you're comfortable before you sign.

The agreement should also set out how and when you can exit the agreement with the agent, if it's not working out. Getting rid of an underperforming agent is easier on a let-only basis and you usually won't need to give much notice. On a full lettings and management contract, you'll probably have to give a month's notice or more. It's just another thing to keep in mind when you look over the contract.

CASE STUDY: UPTON ROAD, WATFORD, HERTFORDSHIRE

The project

Conversion of a hotel to an aparthotel, creating 27 serviced accommodation studio apartments.

The details

We developed this property specifically with the serviced accommodation model in mind, renting out the finished studios on a weekly or monthly basis to the many professionals who were flocking to this area for short-term contracts. We managed the lettings side of things in house, and got to a point where the property was functioning well as serviced accommodation lets, with regular tenants and high occupancy, and earning an annual income of £230,000.

However, our ultimate goal was to sell the whole building as a going concern to an investor buyer.

When marketing the property to buyers, we worked with two agents on a dual-agency agreement. One was a local estate agent and the other was a global agent with a specific focus on marketing ongoing investments to property funds and high net worth individuals. In the end, we sold the property to a Swedish fund for £2.8 million (after buying the original hotel for £1.1 million and spending £400,000 on the development).

The new owners then took over the management of the building and continued to run it as serviced accommodation.

The key takeaway

As this property was being sold as an ongoing investment, working with an investment-focused agent with global reach really paid off. We ultimately attracted a high-value buyer that we probably wouldn't have found in the immediate area.

CHAPTER 10

PROTECTING YOURSELF AGAINST MARKET SWINGS AND UNCERTAINTY

Property is often seen as a lower-risk investment that other asset classes, especially for less-experienced investors. But, as with any investment of your time, money and energy, there's always a risk that it won't pay off. Property markets are subject to swings and prone to uncertainty, just like money markets, and if you want to make a career out of property development - which ultimately means you won't have a 9-5 job to fall back on - you need some practical strategies to manage this.

I'm always wary of the phrase 'future-proof', as nothing is ever truly future-proof, but let's say that's what you're aiming for in theory: to create an income from property that can withstand whatever comes your way further down the line.

In this chapter, I cover my favourite tips and tricks for doing just that, based on my nearly two decades in property - two decades in which I've weathered the 2007/2008 financial crisis (and resulting credit crunch), and the coronavirus crisis.

REMEMBER, ALWAYS ADD VALUE

This was one of the first things I said in this book, but it bears repeating. One of the reasons property development can be so lucrative, regardless of whether you develop to sell or rent, is that you're *adding value* to a property or a piece of land by developing it. You're not just relying on property prices to go up for you make a profit.

PRO TIP

If you can keep the motto 'always add value' in mind, and look for ways to maximise the amount of GDV you're adding to a site, you've got some extra protection already built in to your investment. You'll have opportunities to make money regardless of the wider economic situation.

For example, I might find that I get more GDV by building 42 affordable studio flats instead of 20 luxury two-bedroom apartments, particularly if the local area is full of young professionals struggling to get on the housing market. Ultimately, even if I have to pivot to a different end strategy - for example, if the market shifts, I might need to rent out those studio flats for a while instead of selling them - I still get a very good return on my investment because I've developed for maximum GDV.

In this way, I find that developing for maximum value gives me a greater sense of control. Circle back to Chapter 2 for more on developing with particular strategies in mind and adding maximum value to your developments.

IS PROPERTY DEVELOPMENT BETTER SUITED TO BOOM OR BUST MARKETS?

This is one of the questions novice developers regularly ask me. The honest answer is it can work well in both a rising or falling market, so long as you're prepared to tailor your end strategy to suit the market.

If you're developing to rent, you're generally subject to smaller peaks and troughs in the market, but you will still notice trends. Often when the sales market slows, the rental market ramps up because fewer people are buying and selling (or, in the case of a credit crunch, people simply can't get the finance to buy, so they have no choice but to rent). Likewise, in an absolutely booming market, where house prices are going up rapidly, many buyers at the lower end of the ladder will find themselves priced out and forced to rent for longer.

It's when you're developing to sell that you're more at the mercy of the property market. Which brings me to . . .

Developing in rising markets

In a boom market, where sales prices are on the up, developing to sell obviously works well because you gain added uplift from rising prices (on top of the value that you've added by developing the property).

But developing to sell, even in a strong rising market, isn't without its risks. If you get your timings wrong, or if a sale simply takes longer than you think, you're the one stuck servicing an expensive mortgage or loan and all the bills. Which is why I generally (although not always) develop for rental income more so than developing to sell, regardless of what the market is doing. At the very least, you'll want to have a plan B in mind, so that you know what you'll do if you can't sell quickly, even in a booming market.

Developing in falling or stagnant markets

A weak property market can seriously affect developers who build to sell. The good news is, when you're developing to sell in a declining or stagnant market, you've still usually got an inbuilt buffer because you've added value to the site. (The exception to this rule being when the market undergoes a huge and rapid decline, where your buffer gets eaten up.)

That said, in a downward market, I do think it's better if you have the option to keep the property and rent it out rather than sell at that time - you earn a steady income, plus you're retaining a valuable asset for the future. When I develop for income, I'm usually planning to retain the property for at least five years (sometimes as long as 20 years, depending on the strategy), so the underlying value of the property ultimately has a chance to recover. Therefore, being willing to invest for medium- and long-term income, and not just short-term capital gains, is another good way to protect your portfolio against market changes. (More on diversifying your portfolio coming up.)

PRO TIP

Always have a plan B in mind, and be prepared to switch from a sales strategy to a rental strategy (or vice versa) if the market calls for it.

A declining market can also actively benefit developers. When some people are panicking and selling cheap, you can snap up some great bargains for development. In this way, there's definitely something to be said for going *against* what the rest of the market is doing, especially if you're prepared to invest for the medium or long term (as opposed to trying to develop and sell quickly in a struggling market). At the time of writing this book, for example, coronavirus has wreaked havoc on many businesses and the market for commercial properties is on a downward trend, meaning there are great deals out there for developers who are prepared to look to the long term, or are prepared to convert those properties for a different use altogether.

3 TECHNIQUES FOR DIVERSIFYING YOUR PORTFOLIO

The coronavirus crisis is a perfect example of why you want to diversify your portfolio as much as possible. Maybe you heard horror stories of property investors who owned and operated dozens of Airbnb properties? When the pandemic put a stop to most travel, income from these types of properties dried up overnight and the owners were left servicing huge mortgage debt. It's a nightmare scenario, but one that could have been easily avoided by building an income stream that's as diverse as possible.

PRO TIP

It's never a good idea to rely on one source of income alone.

If you can diversify your property portfolio, you'll be much better placed to withstand market swings and uncertainty. If one part of your portfolio starts to struggle (be it property sales, renting to professionals, Airbnb lets or whatever), the other parts will be able to pick up the slack. This is absolutely vital if you intend to earn a full-time living from property.

My three trusted techniques for building a diverse portfolio are:

- Develop for long-term income as well as short-term capital gains
- Be prepared to cater to different tenant profiles
- Learn other property investment strategies

Let's briefly explore each technique.

Developing for long-term income as well as short-term capital gains

I won't spend a lot of time on this as by now you know that I retain a lot of my developments as rental properties, so that I can generate a steady income. Rental income, coupled with the capital gains from build-to-sell projects, will give you a nicely balanced revenue stream, whatever is happening in the property market.

It's true that operating your development as a rental does require some work (finding and managing tenants, maintaining the property, etc.), plus there is always a risk of void periods (when a property sits empty, not earning an income). But much of the day-to-day work can be outsourced to lettings agents or an individual property manager, assuming you prefer to be more hands-off (see Chapter 9). And void periods are less of an issue when you develop multi-unit or multi-tenant properties (such as blocks of flats or larger HMO properties), as opposed to renting a property out to a single tenant or family.

Catering to different tenant profiles

Keep in mind that you can always inject some diversification into the rental part of your portfolio by renting to different audiences. It's not all about renting to professionals, in other words. Renting to social housing tenants and/or students is a profitable approach for many investors. In fact, in some markets, renting to these different tenant profiles may be a much more sensible approach - for example, if you're developing in a university town, or if wider economic factors mean the market for professional rentals is shaky.

Check out the case study at the end of this chapter to see how renting to different audiences helped my business during the coronavirus crisis.

Learning about other property investment strategies

HMOs, serviced accommodation (short-term lets with hotel-like services), holiday lets, rent to rent, lease options . . . there are lots of ways to make money through property where you don't have to develop the site. (Obviously, some light refurbishment or redecoration may be required, depending on the project).

My portfolio incorporates many of these investment strategies and I encourage you to explore at least one other property strategy besides developing. (If you're interested in exploring other strategies, check out my book *Property Investment Strategies for Beginners* or browse Wealth Lab's educational resources at wealthlabs.co.uk.)

When you have other property investment strategies up your sleeve, you have more options and, ultimately, more control. Say for some reason your development projects stall – which could happen because of something as small as a funding delay or something as huge as a global pandemic. Doesn't it make sense to have at least one other property investment strategy to fall back on?

PRO TIP

You may even find that these different strategies eventually feed into your development projects. That's certainly been the case for me – I started by renting out some small HMO houses, and have since developed whole apartment buildings into HMO flats. I've also developed specifically for serviced accommodation use.

Now, I'm not saying you should go out and try six different property strategies all at once. I use a number of different property investment strategies, but I learnt them one at a time, taking up to a year to really master each one. Only ever attempt one new strategy at a time, and really get to grips with it before you're tempted to incorporate another new strategy into your portfolio.

TOP BUSINESS TIPS FOR RIDING OUT MARKET CHALLENGES

Here, I'd like to share a few other miscellaneous tips, tricks and methods – things that are more business- and mindset-related than specifically about property, but have nonetheless helped me cope with market challenges and create a reliable, robust income from property.

In Chapter 11 you'll see that I find business and entrepreneurship books really inspiring. I urge you to get curious and learn from other successful businesspeople, not just property people. After all, pretty much every successful entrepreneur has overcome some sort of business challenge or adversity along the way, which means you can learn lots from them about building resilience. (That goes for business and personal resilience, by the way.)

This section is in no way an exhaustive list of how to overcome challenges – more, it's a collection of lessons that have really resonated with and helped me over the years.

Let's get into it.

Be better than the rest

To put it bluntly, it's easy to take risks and make money in a buoyant market. Any old schmuck can do that. The really smart developers and investors are those who can make money in *any* market.

So when things get tough, you have to be prepared to work 10 times harder than your competitors, especially those who just piled in for the easy money. You have to be smarter than them. And you have to be braver than them. Which brings me to . . .

Hold your (financial) nerve

When the economy stutters, businesses react in one of two ways. They either pull up the drawbridge and look for ways to save money – often by reducing investment in things like marketing, research, product development, new hires. Or they hold their nerve and continue to invest and work towards their strategic goals.

Often, the second type of business isn't just able to hold fast in an economic crisis, they often *gain* market share, precisely because their competitors are having less impact. In my business, then, I continue to spend on things like marketing when others might be thinking about tightening their belts. In other words, I don't take my foot off the gas.

Don't be afraid of change

Be honest, do you see change as a force for good, something that motivates you to evolve, adapt and do better? Or do you see change as a negative, something that usually leaves you distracted, disengaged and demotivated?

Whether it's market changes, personnel changes within my businesses, or whatever, I try to get excited about change. I try to see it as an opportunity to evolve and innovate. Sure, it's not always easy to see it this way. If your default position is to be wary of change, you'll probably have to work hard to intentionally look for the positives. But if you can learn to embrace change - and I believe any trait can be *learnt* - you'll have something in common with the most successful business leaders in the world.

Be nimble

Part of embracing change is being willing to try new things. This is especially true when something just isn't working for you. If a strategy isn't paying off or delivering your goals, don't stubbornly cling to it, hoping it'll work out next time, or the time after that.

Equally, if something has done *very well* for you in the past, but the market has since shifted, why bother clinging onto something that no longer works? Those investors operating multiple Airbnbs spring to mind here - it's a strategy that may have worked brilliantly in the past, but it won't work well at all during a global pandemic. In cases like this, you need to react to the market. Switch to a different model. Target a different audience. Change things up, basically.

Speed is important here, too. The quicker you react, the more likely you are to successfully weather market shifts.

Invest in your personal brand

Raising your personal profile can really help your business grow and succeed, whatever is happening in the wider market. As an example, I grow my personal brand by writing about property, creating property-related video content for YouTube, appearing on property TV, and generally putting myself out there as an expert in my field.

Because of this, I find more diverse opportunities come my way. Investors started approaching me about mentoring them through developments, and this has now become an important part of my business. And when editors at the global *For Dummies* brand were looking for a UK businessperson to write a book about Brexit, they came to me. These aren't avenues I would have necessarily aimed for in my career, back when I was starting out - they happened organically because I'd invested in my personal brand, and they turned out to be hugely rewarding and fun. Plus, as an added bonus, it all feeds back into boosting my brand.

You don't have to write books or create videos to build your own brand. There are lots of ways to raise your profile and demonstrate your expertise. You could, for example:

- Contribute to forums and online groups
- Write articles and publish them on LinkedIn
- Be active on social media, such as sharing property development tips and success stories from projects
- Create free downloadable guides to key property development topics
- Write and promote your own weekly email newsletter (which is great because then you build your own mailing list)
- Offer to speak at local events
- Mentor people who are interested in entering the industry
- Engage with others in the industry and generally expand your network as much as you can

Automate or outsource business processes where you can

Across all industries, automation is a huge topic, so this is a good thing to keep in mind as your business expands. All sorts of business processes can be automated with software, spanning marketing, sales, finance and more. I'm constantly reviewing my business processes to see which tasks can be done quicker, cheaper and easier through software. For example, we use customer relationship management (CRM) software to handle much of our back-end marketing and sales tasks, such as logging interactions with customers.

In my mind, outsourcing work to freelancers also falls under this banner, since it's still about taking tasks off your plate so you can focus your time and expertise where it matters most. Doing your own bookkeeping is a classic example of a trap that lots of self-employed people fall into. They think it saves money, but really it's taking precious time away from other more important tasks that genuinely add value. Outsourcing stuff like this is money well spent.

This feeds back into the passive income mindset that I referenced earlier this book. You can't do everything yourself. Why would you want to, especially when, according to the famous 80/20 rule, 80% of results come from 20% of effort? Far better to focus your time and energy on the 20% of activity that really delivers the results you want (income, successful outcomes to your projects, etc.) and outsource or automate the other 80%.

CASE STUDY: REDBRICK HOUSE, NEWBURY, BERKSHIRE

The project

Commercial office to residential conversion creating 42 micro-studios.

The details

This was a build-to-rent strategy, where my company retained the building and rented the 42 units to young professionals. However, when the coronavirus crisis hit, some of my rental income from young professionals was adversely affected.

So I switched up my strategy and turned 30% of the building over to social housing. Many investors are wary of renting to social housing tenants, but it's a growing model. (In other words, it's a good strategy to keep an eye on, even if it doesn't immediately appeal to you at this stage in your career.)

Crucially, the social housing rent was paid directly by the local council, so I didn't have to worry about chasing up individual tenants for late rent. (The perception that social housing tenants are unreliable payers is a common sticking point that puts a lot of investors off this strategy.) Renting to the local council also meant they managed the nitty gritty of placing tenants in the units, and covered any void periods.

The rental income was strong, too - in fact, not far off the rental income from professional lets.

There's a key caveat to bear in mind, though, and that is it's usually not a great idea to mix different tenant profiles in the same building (mixing professionals and students, for example, or professionals and social housing).

In this case, the risk with turning 30% of units over to social housing tenants is that the building would then become less desirable for my existing professional tenants, whom I very much wanted to keep happy. Luckily, there was a simple solution. The ground floor of Redbrick House has its own entrance, which meant it could be easily let to the council for social housing, without impacting the rest of the building. The professional tenants and social housing tenants didn't mix and only ever had access to their own part of the building.

Of course, if the building wasn't conducive to mixing tenants, an alternative approach would have been to switch the whole building over to social housing.

The key takeaway

Injecting some diversification into your portfolio and creating multiple revenue streams from different sources is a good way to ride out market challenges. That can mean creating a balanced lettings portfolio that caters to different audiences.

CHAPTER 11

TAPPING INTO EDUCATION SOURCES

Speaking from experience, you'll never arrive at a point where you feel like you've learnt everything there is to know about property development. There are always new strategies to explore, new market trends to get to grips with, new regulatory requirements, changes to planning laws, etc. So if you're looking for a career where you can continually grow and challenge yourself, you've come to the right place. It's one of the things I love most about property development, and property investment in general - these constant opportunities to learn new things and grow (and I mean grow on a personal level as well as growing my business).

WHY YOU NEED TO PRIORITISE YOUR OWN EDUCATION

I firmly believe that the best thing you can do to level up your property development game, and take it from an on-the-side gig to a viable career, is to invest in your own continuing development.

You have to be prepared to put the work in, though. There's no such thing as a free lunch, as the saying goes, so continual improvement requires some commitment. At the very least It requires an investment of your time and, often, your money.

It can be tricky to prioritise time and funds for things like buying (and reading!) books, completing online learning courses, going to national exhibitions, attending networking groups, and so on. It always seems like there are more pressing things to do - whether that pressure comes from family commitments, working on your development projects or (if you have one) maintaining your day job.

I get it. It's something I struggle with myself. I've got a young family, run my own businesses, and am constantly spinning multiple plates. But I know that taking time out to work on my own education is vital for achieving my goals and building the life I want, for myself and my family.

Mostly, I manage this by carving out time each day to work on my professional development, and I do this first thing in the morning before the kids get up and the day gets crazy. How I spend that time will vary from day to day, depending on what my current focus is. One morning I might be catching up on industry news or researching a new type of strategy. The next morning, I might be trying out a new time management technique or listening to a guided meditation that sets me up for a day of success. It's all growth as far as I'm concerned.

WHERE TO LOOK FOR PROPERTY EDUCATION

One thing that attracts many people to property development is the lack of educational or qualification barriers. Anyone, regardless of background, can make a success of it. Which is

great, but it does mean the educational path maybe isn't as clear and formal as it is for other careers. In other words, you should be prepared to tap into a wide array of educational sources. Here, I list my favourites.

Books

There is a wealth of great content out there for property developers, from step-by-step property development guidance to specific developer strategies. Not all of these are full-sized books; short and snappy ebooks can be a manageable way to delve into a topic. Plus, there are lots of business and entrepreneurship books to get your teeth into.

PRO TIP

If you struggle to find time to read, I highly recommend listening to audiobooks. You can listen to inspiring and educational content while you're traveling to and from work, walking the dog, running or working out, and even stacking the dishwasher. You'd be amazed how much content you can notch up over the course of the day. And if audiobooks aren't you're thing, you might like to subscribe to Blinkist, which provides easy-to-digest summaries of thousands of non-fiction books.

YouTube

The quality of free educational content on YouTube can be incredible – from general business and entrepreneurship advice right down to mastering super-specific techniques, such as maximising your GDV through parking income.

Check out a few property gurus on YouTube and subscribe to those you like best (that way, you get a notification when new videos come out). And in case you're wondering, I do have my own YouTube channel (simply search 'Nicholas Wallwork' on YouTube and you'll find me). I hope to see you on there.

Online community platforms and forums

These are another great source of free advice and training resources. By hanging out on free community platforms and forums you can connect with other developers and investors, spot up-and-coming strategies and get help with specific queries. I recommend wealthlabs.co.uk, which is a free-to-join online wealth-building community with a vast array of property training resources and an extensive network of property professionals. (Full discloser, I co-founded the platform, so let me do the BBC thing and state that other platforms and forums are available!)

PRO TIP

Because I'm passionate about education, there's a section on the Wealth Labs website dedicated to free property education sources, including courses and online events. Head to wealthlabs.co.uk for the latest recommendations and links to useful external sources.

Industry news

If you haven't already, make sure you sign up to newsletters from relevant industry blogs, forums and websites. This is an easy and free way to keep up with industry news.

Another good way is to attend the many national and regional property shows that take place each year. These are great for spotting trends, picking up on industry news and expanding your network. The same goes for relevant networking groups – basically, anything that immerses you more deeply in the property industry is time well spent.

Online courses

There are some excellent online learning platforms out there, such as Udemy (who I've previously partnered with to create a property course), Coursera, LearnDirect and of course, Wealth Labs. These sources are often most useful for learning more about overall strategies, rather than nitty gritty, step-by-step guidance - simply because the authors of these courses may be based outside of the UK and may be subject to a whole different set of property regulations. If you need UK-specific guidance, make sure that's what you're signing up for.

Mentorship

If you can find a more experienced developer to mentor you, you'll be able to benefit from their wisdom and learn from their mistakes. I cannot stress enough how valuable this is.

Mentorship can mean anything from an ad hoc coffee and catchup with a more experience developer than you, to structured weekly mentorship sessions that cover specific topics. It all comes down to what works for you and your mentor.

The catch is, it can be hard to find a property developer mentor - particularly if other developers see you as an up-and-coming competitor. (Some people care about this more than others. Personally, I'm of the opinion there are plenty of good deals to go around.)

If you are struggling to connect with a mentor, then a formal, paid-for mentorship arrangement can be a great option. I now spend quite a bit of my time mentoring property developers and investors in one-to-one sessions, and will even help them to complete a development project. (If this sort of mentorship arrangement appeals to you, head to wealthlabs. co.uk and search the navigation bar for *Nicholas Wallwork Mentorships* for more info.)

PRO TIP

As an alternative to working with a property development mentor, consider working with a general business mentor. For example, you might feel you could learn more from someone who has built a successful business from the ground up, or built a hugely successful personal brand online. Mentors come in all shapes and sizes.

DON'T FORGET ABOUT INSPIRATION, AS WELL AS EDUCATION

Finally, as well as working on your property education, be sure to pay attention to your personal development. I mentioned meditation earlier in the chapter, and you might have raised an eyebrow wondering what on earth that's got to do with being a successful property developer. My answer is, I'm here for anything that helps me be a better business person, whether that means learning to be more productive, be less stressed, be more focused, manage my time better, achieve a great work-life balance, whatever.

PRO TIP

Property development is just another form of entrepreneurship. Strip away the property stuff and it's all about doing something you love, building a successful business, working for yourself, escaping the rat race and turning your passion into a career. You can learn a lot from other people who have managed to do the same, whatever their industry.

Which is probably why I'm addicted to reading (or listening to) books about entrepreneurship and autobiographies of successful people. I've also found a lot of useful nuggets in books at the more self-help end of the spectrum, and now incorporate things like positive affirmations and mindfulness into my daily routine. If this sounds a little airy fairy, it's not. All of this content has given me practical tools that genuinely benefit my business.

In other words, don't close off any avenue that may help you progress as a property developer. Keep an open mind, cultivate a mindset of constant curiosity and be willing to invest in yourself and your future. It'll be one of the smartest investments you'll ever make.

Printed in Great Britain
by Amazon

46594777R00116